Some Philosophical Issues in
Logic and Language

Some Philosophical Issues in
Logic and Language

Sadhan Chakraborti

Suryodaya Books

Cataloging in Publication Data — DK
[Courtesy: D.K. Agencies (P) Ltd. <docinfo@dkagencies.com>]

Chakraborti, Sadhan, author.
Some philosophical issues in logic and language / Sadhan Chakraborti.
pages cm
Includes bibliographical references.
ISBN: 9788192611457

1. Logic. 2. Language and languages – Philosophy. I. Title. II. Title: Logic and language.

BC108.C43 2016 DDC 160 23

ISBN: 978-81-926114-5-7
First published in India in 2016

Published by:
Department of Philosophy
Jadavpur University
Kolkata - 700 032

and

Suryodaya Books
"Suryodaya", D-36A/1, Mohan Garden
Najafgarh Road, New Delhi - 110 059
Phone: (011) 2535 3435

Distributed by:
D.K. Printworld (P) Ltd.
Regd. Office: "Vedaśrī", F-395, Sudarshan Park
(Metro Station: Ramesh Nagar), New Delhi - 110 015
Phones: (011) 2545 3975, 2546 6019; *Fax*: (011) 2546 5926
e-mail: indology@dkprintworld.com
Website: www.dkprintworld.com

Printed by: Suryodaya Books, New Delhi

Preface

THE interrelation between logic and language transpires when we delve into some philosophical issues arising from logic or from language. This collection of essays captures some aspects of the interrelation between logic and language. The development of my philosophical thoughts has been reflected in this collection, including those articles written by me at different points of my philosophical trajectory.

Chapter 1 elaborates two versions of triple negation, a logical principle. One version is found in the intuitionistic logic and the other version is found in the Nyāya system, belonging to an Indian philosophical school. Each version of the logical principle is couched in the concerned language. $\sim\sim\sim p \longleftrightarrow \sim p$ (triple negation) is admitted in the intuitionistic logic as a logical principle. It is also admitted in Navya-Nyāya system. The essay is an expository account of the logical principle of triple negation found in these two systems.

The notion of truth plays a very important role in various aspects of philosophy of language. There are some serious misconceptions about the Dummettian notion of truth and its place in his philosophy of language. The aim of Chapter 2 is to give an authentic account of the Dummettian notion of truth and the role it plays in his philosophy of language.

Chapter 3 aims at examining whether A.J. Ayer is a phenomenalist or not. It is commonly believed that Ayer is a phenomenalist. The essay formulates Ayer's two-tier theory of language, specifically of the language consisting of statements concerning physical objects; clarifies the meaning of phenomenalism and finally shows that it is a wrong supposition that Ayer is a phenomenalist and this is shown in the backdrop of his two-tier theory of language.

Chapter 4 deals with the demarcation of the study concerning what is said and the study concerning what is meant in linguistic communication, if there be any. The former one is usually known as semantics and the latter as pragmatics.

Chapter 5 elaborates Jerry A. Fodor's position in the context of holism–realism debate. Fodor has made an attempt to undermine semantic holism. He has tried to show that the arguments on the basis of which semantic holism has actually been proposed cannot establish it. He proposes an alternative semantics for the intentional states. This essay shows that the whole project of Fodor is ill founded.

The problem of justifying deduction is a perennial one. Chapter 6 gives a sketch of the alternative solutions to the problem of justifying deduction formulated by Michael Dummett. It also includes the solution suggested by Pranab Kumar Sen. It makes a critical estimate of the suggested solutions to the problem by Dummett and Sen. Finally, it shows that the success of any of these competing views depends upon establishing which kind of theory of meaning is a legitimate one.

Chapter 7 states in clear terms what the computational theory of mind is. It is a theory of mind developed by cognitive scientists, who claim to give a scientific account of mental processes that determine human intelligent activities. Learning a language is one of the human intelligent activities. The chapter gives a description of the architecture of mind or cognition, from the perspective of cognitive scientists' computational theory of mind, that regulates human linguistic behaviour.

Chapter 8 addresses the issue of objectivity of mathematical and logic statements in the context of Wittgenstein's philosophy. The issue dealt with here has two components:

i. Deciphering the nuances involved in the concept of

objectivity of statements and giving a clearer idea of the objectivity of mathematical and logical statements, and

ii. whether Wittgenstein admits objectivity of mathematical statements. Commentators of Wittgenstein differ on the question whether Wittgenstein was a realist about mathematics and logic or not.

The essay "Wittgenstein on Necessity and Objectivity in Mathematics and Logic" attempts to establish that according to Wittgenstein, logico-mathematical statements are necessary and objective; since Wittgenstein advocates necessity and objectivity of logical and mathematical statements he should be regarded as a realist.

Chapter 9 deals with the Davidson–Dummett controversy over the issue of explaining the meaning of the sentences of a language in terms of truth conditions. The Davidsonian theory of meaning is attacked by Dummett. The essay aims at giving a defence of the Davidsonian truth conditions theory of meaning against the Dummettian attack.

Chapter 10 aims at deciphering the aspects of understanding a person's utterance. It attempts to enumerate the different aspects involved in understanding a language used by a person and for each aspect certain conditions are fulfilled, which makes our understanding of the language of the person possible. It gives an outline of the conditions associated with the hearer's understanding of the speaker's utterance, the fulfilment of which make it possible.

If we say that speakers use language to describe how the world is then one may ask the question what is the relation between a language and the world? A further question that arises from this answer is – how is it possible for a language to represent the world?

An attempt has been made in Chapter 11 to show that the recent neuro-scientific studies provide a ground to the claim that the neural system of humans put the limit to our knowledge of the external world. If this claim is true then the distal theory of linguistic representation cannot stand.

The long tradition of considering the concept of truth as one of the most important subjects of philosophical discussion has been questioned by many philosophers in contemporary philosophical discourse. The reaction ranges from giving truth an improper role to abolishing it from the philosophical arena. Examining some of the reasons behind this range of reactive theses and showing the folly of trying to tarnish truth constitute the aim of Chapter 12.

There are different views regarding the nature of empathy, a process of knowing the mental worlds of others. Some researchers hold that it is a form of analogical thinking. Chapter 13 refutes this view and tries to establish reasoning as a form of abduction.

Contents

1

Two Faces of Triple Negation

In his illuminating and thought-provoking paper Kalikrishna Banerjee[1] has explained clearly the logic of Navya-Nyāya philosophers in contrast with that of early-Nyāya philosophers. In doing this, of course, he has not confined himself to the logics of these two groups of philosophers. He has also elaborated the ontological divergences of these two groups in the background of which the difference in their logics can be clearly understood. His inquiry has not stopped even with this — he has explained the reasons for their ontological divergences. Let us first note the differences between these two schools of Nyāya in their respective logics and ontologies as pointed out by Banerjee. In logics the difference between the old and the new Naiyāyikas lies in that the early-Nyāya philosophers admit the law of double negation, i.e. the law "$--p \leftrightarrow p$", where p is any statement whatsoever; but the Navya-Nyāya philosophers do not admit the law of double negation although they admit the law of triple negation, i.e. the law "$---p \leftrightarrow p$". The relevant ontological difference is that the Navya-Nyāya ontology is more encompassing: it admits more abstract entities like a second negative fact (*abhāvābhāva*), its coordinate negatum and so on. These entities do not find any place in early-Nyāya ontology. It did not escape the notice of Banerjee that the peculiarity of the Navya-Nyāya logic, i.e. a rejection of the law of double negation together with an admission of the principle of triple negation, is shared by the intuitionistic logic, a strong mathematical logic. The ingenuity of Banerjee culminates in bringing out the differences between the Navya-Nyāya logic and the intuitionistic

1 See Banerjee, 1979, "The Doctrine of Triple Negation in Neo-Nyaya Logic".

logic.[2] After mentioning some points of difference between these two logics he says that there are many other points of difference as well, the explanation of which he reserves for a separate paper. My humble aim here is to undertake this unfinished task in the light of my respected teacher's thought.

I shall discuss first the points of difference mentioned by Banerjee between logics of these two kinds and shall then try to bring out some other differences which will make explicit the logics and the philosophies of the Navya-Naiyāyikas and intuitionists. In doing this, however, I am accepting without question whatever is said by Banerjee about the logic and the metaphysics of Navya-Nyāya.

The first difference pointed out by Banerjee is that while developing their logic the Navya-Naiyāyikas were interested in entities whereas the intuitionists were interested in statements. It is not quite clear to me what is meant by a logic of entities. Logic is usually understood as being concerned primarily with inference, more specifically, with the validity of inference. The validity of an inference is understood in terms of a certain relation between its premises which are statements or sentences or propositions[3] and its conclusion which is again a statement or a sentence or a proposition. We can say that this relation holds between the premises and the conclusion of an inference if the inference preserves the truth of its premises in its conclusion, i.e. it is such that whenever its premises are all true the conclusion is also true. Validity is sometimes defined, not in terms of truth, but in purely syntactic terms. We are not considering it because it is not in accordance with what we usually mean by "valid". Thus we see that since logic is concerned primarily with the validity of an inference and since validity itself is a matter of a certain relation between the premises and fhe conclusion of an inference which are after all statements, we can obviously say that logic is concerned with statements which are truth bearers. So, it is

[2] Banerjee, 1979, op. cit., p. 193, n. 65.

[3] Here I am consciously obliterating the distinctions made between sentence, statement and proposition in order to avoid complexity.

not clear how entities, which are not truth bearers, can be what a logic is concerned with. There is a view, however, that propositions, which are truth bearers are also entities. But I am sure that Banerjee is not considering entities of this kind while saying that Navya-Nyāya logicians were interested in entities.

It seems that Banerjee was aware of this difficulty and so admitted a possibility of treating Navya-Nyāya logic as concerned with statements. This can possibly be understood in the following manner. In a concrete situation whenever we consider an "absence of a thing" (*abhāva*) we consider it by relating it to a locus, e.g. we say the floor has the absence of a jar on it (*ghatābhāvavat bhūtalam*) which can be represented as "It is not the case that the floor has a jar on it", which is the negation of the statement "the floor has a jar on it". When the early Naiyāyika says that the absence of the absence of *ghata* is identical with *ghata*, he can represent it in terms of statements as the statement it is not the case that it is not the case that the floor has a jar on it is equivalent to the floor has a jar on it, i.e. to put it schematically, $--p\leftrightarrow p$, where p is any statement whatsoever. So, we can say that even Navya-Naiyāyikas were concerned with statements while developing their logic. Even if the Navya-Nyāya logic is treated as a logic of statements we can exhibit its difference from that of intuitionists, says Banerjee, on at least two other grounds. One ground as pointed out by Banerjee, quoting a passage from the writing of Gadādhara, is that since Navya-Naiyāyikas admit that "p" and "$-p$" are opposed, so they have to admit "$p\rightarrow--p$ and "$--p\rightarrow p$". But intuitionists cannot admit these two implications. I am not going to discuss this remark but would only say that it seems puzzling because it is not clear if these implications are admitted by the Navya-Naiyāyikas — how can they say that the second negation is additional? Admission of these two implications seems to imply that the second negation is identical with the negatum of the first negation and so not additional.

Another ground is that the Navya-Nyāya semantics is two-valued whereas the intuitionistic semantics is three-valued.[4] In other

[4] See Banerjee, op. cit, p. 193, n. 65 and pp. 193-94.

words, the Navya-Nyāya logicians admit just two statement values whereas the intuitionists admit three statement values. There can, however, be a dispute over this observation of Banerjee. This observation has two parts — one is that the Navya-Nyāya semantics is two-valued and the other is that the intuitionistic semantics is three-valued. There cannot be any dispute over the first part of the observation, but the second part can be disputed. Although it is true that there is no standard intuitionistic semantics Heyting's explanation of intuitionism[5] is usually regarded as an explanation incorporating the basic insights of intuitionism. Heyting holds that a mathematical proposition p always demands a mathematical construction with certain properties which constitute a proof of it.[6] If this construction exists or if we are in possession of this construction then we can assert it; if such a construction does not exist or if we are not in possession of it then we cannot assert it. Heyting admits that given a statement p, either we possess a construction or a method of yielding a construction which proves p or we do not possess it. Now for Heyting our possessing a proof of a statement p is the same as the statement's being true.[7] Similarly if we do not possess a proof of p then we can also say that p is false. Heyting says: $\vdash(\forall x)p(x)$ (i.e. $(\forall x)\, pc(x)$ can be asserted) means that $P(x)$ is true for every x in the domain Q; in other words, we possess a general method of construction which, if any element a of Q is chosen, yields by specialization the construction $P(a)$.[8] Thus we see that even in intuitionistic semantics the number of statement values is two, i.e. intuitionistic semantics is not really three-valued. We can get a confirmation of this claim in Kripke's semantics for intuitionistic logic.[9] While defining an intuitionistic model on a model structure $(G, K, R,)$ he clearly mentions that the set of

---

5 See Heyting, 1971, *Intuitionism.*

6 Ibid., p. 102.

7 For the intuitionist to possess a construction which proves p is the same as possessing a proof of pp. 106-07.

8 See Heyting, op. cit., p 106.

9 Cf. Kripke, 1965, "Semantical Analysis of Intuitionistic Logic I", pp. 92-130.

statement values is $\{T, F\}$.

An (intuitionistic) model on a model structure (G, K, R) is a binary function ϕ (P, H), where P ranges over arbitrary propositional letters and H ranges over elements of K whose range is the set $\{T, \mathrm{F}\}$.[10]

Thus we see that one has reason to dispute Banerjee's remark that intuitionistic semantics is three-valued still Banerjee had a point when he made this remark. The point is that the intuitionistic semantics does not admit the principle of bivalence; but this principle is retained in the Navya-Nyāya semantics. Bivalence, however, should not be confused with two-valuedness. A two-valued semantics can very well deny the principle of bivalence. The principle of bivalence is that every statement is either determinately true or determinately false. One of the possibilities of the failure of this principle is due to vagueness. The failure of bivalence in intuitionistic semantics is not of this kind. It rather relates to the peculiarity of the intuitionistic notion of truth. This is possible, however, only if the notion of truth is defined in a way different from that of a realist. This point can be made clear if we can give examples of statements where the principle of bivalence does not apply although the two-valuedness is retained. I will come to this point very soon after explaining the non-realistic notion of truth. So I am postponing this task for a while. The root of the difference between the two semantic theories lies in the difference between the notion of truth in Navya-Nyāya semantics and that of intuitionistic semantics. In Navya-Nyāya semantics truth is not possibly identified with assertability; but intuitionistic semantics identifies truth with assertability. I am not going to explain the notion of "truth as found in Navya-Nyāya semantics. Probably the idea of *tadvātītaprakārakatva* explains the notion of truth here. If this is true then it is not essentially different from a correspondence theory as catered in Tarski's theory of truth.[11] I am rather explaining the notion of truth as found in intuitionistic semantics.

---

10 Cf. Kripke, 1965, op. cit., p. 94.

11 Cf. Tarski, 1956, "The concept of Truth in Formalised Languages".

Michael Dummett has made an attempt to define the notion of truth in the intuitionistic manner.[12] Let us consider his definition of truth. Dummett has modified the definition of truth in different stages. In his final version he says that an intuitionist can say that a mathematical statement is true iff there exists a proof of it.[13] Here the word "exist" is to be understood intuitionistically. For the intuitionist "there exists a proof of a mathematical statement" means that a mathematical construction can be given which counts as a proof of it. While giving the final version of his definition of truth he says that an intuitionist need not say that a (mathematical) proposition *A* is true iff we have proved *A*. He should rather say that *A* is true iff we are able to prove *A*. In other words, *A* is true iff we possess, or are able to give, a construction which proves *A*. If there exists a proof for a statement to the effect that we cannot have a mathematical construction which counts as a proof of it then the sentence is false. So, for the intuitionist if a sentence is not true, i.e, if we cannot have a mathematical construction which counts as a proof of it it is tantamount to its being false. So the principle of *tertium non-datur*, i.e. the principle that no statement is neither true nor false is sustained. This shows that the intuitionistic logic is not a logic of truth-value gap, the kind of logic we associate with Strawson's idea of presupposition. Intuitionists do not admit any meaningful statement which is neither true nor false. But it should be very clear that the intuitionistic notion of truth does not allow the principle of bivalence, i.e. the principle that every statement is either determinately true or determinately false. Because there are certain statements for which we have not yet been able to make any mathematical construction which counts as a proof of their or under which statements of this kind are assertable. Let us call these sentences "so far undecidable sentences". So, we cannot say that these statements are true. Neither can we say that they are false. Because uptil now we fail to prove that we cannot have such a construction. Neither can we assert them nor can we deny them.

---

[12] Cf. Dummett, 1982, "Realism".

[13] See ibid., p. 91; and Dummatt, 1977, *Elements of Intuitionism*, p. 19.

So, the principle of bivalence does not hold for them. In this context let us consider an example considered by Niel Tennant.[14] The example taken by Tennant is Goldbach's conjecture, viz. that for every even number n greater than 2, there are prime numbers p, q such that $n = (p + q)$. A mathematical construction would constitute a proof of this statement if it provides two constructions of primes p, q such that their addition is 4 (this is the basis); and provides an effective procedure for constructing two primes p, q, such that their addition is $2k$, if two constructions of primes p, q, are given such that their addition is $2\ (k–1)$, where $k > 1$. But this statement (Goldbach's conjecture) is so far undecidable. Neither can we show that such a proof can be constructed nor can we show that it cannot be constructed. But this does not mean that it is impossible to prove or impossible to refute it. "Undecidable" means that we do not at present possess (an effective method for finding) either a proof or a disproof of it. So the participle of bivalence does not apply to it. We can still say that the two-valuedness is retained, because the intuitionistic semantics retains the principle of *tertium non-datur* which we have already seen.

So far, we have seen that the difference between Navya-Nyāya logic and intuitionistic logic is rooted in their corresponding semantics. Dummett has rightly pointed out that the most important task for a philosopher is to choose the semantic theory, i.e. the theory of truth.[15] It is also the most momentous step: it is this choice which has repercussions both on which logical laws we should hold as valid and on which metaphysical views we ought to favour. So, the intuitionistic logic is the result of the above semantic theory of the intuitionists — Similarly the semantic theory, which the Navya-Nyāya philosophers advocated, results in the Navya-Nyāya logic. Again, it is the difference between the two semantic theories of these two groups of philosophers which exhibit the philosophical or ontological difference between them.

The semantic theory of the Navya-Naiyāyikas shows that they

[14] See Tennant, 1987, *Anti-Realism and Logic.*

[15] Cf. Dummett, 1991, *The Logical Basis of Metaphysics.*

are external realists regarding the nature of reality; they think that reality is external and independent and it is reality which makes a statement true. Intuitionists on the other hand, cannot be said to be realists. But they are not idealists either. Dummett calls them anti-realists. Idealism is only a version of anti-realism but not the only version of it. Intuitionism, a version of anti-realism, does not reject a reality waiting to be discovered. Intuitionists rather understand the world as something that is brought into existence by our investigations in a way that is imposed on us from without.[16] They understand the world[17] as something conceptually determined in terms of our recognitional capacity and therefore there is of course a sense in which the world is not already there independently of us. On the other hand, when truth is understood tenselessly it seems that we are admitting that a sentence was already true, as if true, before we showed it to be true. Dag Prawitz puts the intuitionistic understanding of the world thus:

> The world is not there independently of us, but given that we are here, the world is also there waiting to be discovered.[18]

The above world-view of the intuitionists comes very close to the internal realism as propounded by Hilary Putnam.[19]Although it is doubtful whether they are identical or not it seems true that both of these world-views emerge from the elimination of noumena from the Kantian world-view.

It is the above view of semantics which led the intuitionists to construct their logic in the way they have done. Let us take an example. They think that a statement can be admitted if we possess a method by which we can give the construction demanded by it. Thus the logical statement 4 *p v* demands a general method of

---

16 Cf. Dummett, 1978b, "Truth", p. 18.

17 Although by "world" the intuitionists meant originally the mathematical world, later on it has been generalized to the world as such by many philosophers who have affinity to intuitionism.

18 Prawitz, 1987, "Dummett on a Theory of Meaning", p. 154.

19 Cf. Putnam, 1988, *"Many Faces of Realism"*.

construction by which we can give either a proof of p or a proof of $-p$.

Since we do not possess such a general method of construction the intuitionists cannot admit this logical statement in their logic. The rejection of "$--p \rightarrow p$" is made on the same ground.[20] Again the law of triple negation is admitted on the ground that we possess a method of construction by which we can give the construction demanded by the logical statement "$---p \rightarrow -p$". The rejection of the law of double negation and acceptance of the law of triple negation are made by the Navya-Naiyāyikas on the basis of their own semantics which is very different from that of the intuitionists. Thus we see that although the Navya-Naiyāyikas and the intuitionists converge to the point of rejecting the law of double negation and accepting the law of triple negation, their views bear different significance.

Note

This paper is an attempt to remove the vaccum felt by my teacher Prof. K.K. Banerjee in his insightful paper "The Doctrine of Triple Negation in Neo-Nyaya Logic", in *Logic Ontology and Action*, Jadavpur Studies in Philosophy, vol. I, general editor K.K. Banerjee, Delhi: Macmillan 1979.

---

[20] Cf. Heyting, op. cit., p. 104.

2

Michael Dummett on Truth

MICHAEL Dummett subscribes to a verificationist[1] theory of meaning for natural language which is a generalization of the intuitionist's theory of meaning for the language of mathematics. Again he advocates intuitionistic logic which, he thinks, is a consequence of this anti-realism, a semantic theory, as described by him. In all of these three different aspects of his philosophy of language — (a) in the theory of meaning, (b) in logic, and (c) in the semantic theory — the notion of truth plays a very important role. Dummett's views in these different fields are ultimately rooted in the notion of truth introduced by him as opposed to the classical notion of truth. There are some serious misconceptions about the Dummettian notion of truth and its place in his philosophy of language which are again roots of many other misconceptions about his philosophy of language. My aim in this chapter is to explain what exactly the Dummettian notion of truth is and the role it plays in his philosophy of language.

A popular reading of Dummett's theory of meaning and the place of the notion of truth in it is that Dummett advocates a verificationist theory of meaning — a theory of meaning in which the central place is not occupied by truth but by verification. But we shall see that this reading is suspect.

While criticizing the Truth conditions Theory of Meaning (henceforth TTM) Dummett says:

> The question before us is whether the concept of truth is the right choice for the central notion of a theory of meaning . . . .[2]

---

1 Verification is a generalized concept of the concept of proof in mathematics.

2 Dummett, 1976, "What Is a Theory of Meaning? (II)", p. 75.

TTM in which the notion of truth is the central notion has been vehemently criticized by Dummett. To understand Dummett's real charge against the TTM we should start with what Dummett thinks about the interrelation between the different aspects of the philosophy of language — the theory of meaning (sense), semantics (or the theory of truth/reference) and logic, because the significance of his charge lies in some results from this interconnection and this interconnection constitutes the background for comprehending the role of truth in his philosophy of language. He emphasizes that part of semantics to which he thinks the question of realism is related. So, let us put, very briefly, Dummett's semantic interpretation of it first and then come back to the interrelation between the different aspects of his philosophy of language in the background of which his charge against TTM can be understood. Dummett's critique of TTM leads him to advocate the view he puts forth regarding the nature of the notion of truth and its place in his theory of meaning.

Dummett thinks that the term "realism" is not a blanket term. The question of realism arises only with respect to a given class of something,[3] allowing thereby a possibility of one's being realist in one field and not in another which is almost undisputed in recent thinking. The traditional metaphysicians want to regard them as entities and dispute over the question whether or not they really exist in the world. So it may be labelled as "entity realism". This class may consist, on this veiw, of material objects, mathematical entities, universals and so on. They used to say that realism concerning a given class of entities is the belief that these objects exist independently of our knowing them. This is a material mode of presenting the matter. The formal mode which is also in vogue is that this class consists of terms. So, realism concerning a class of terms is the belief that the elements of this class have genuine references. Dummett contends that this formulation of realism in both of these modes is inadequate and misleaing. There

---

[3] This class with respect to which the dispute over realism arises is called by Dummett "the disputed class".

are some fields where the dispute arises meaningfully but the dispute over realism cannot be formulated in these fields if realism likes the form of entity realism. Realism in morality, realism about the past are among such fields. We cannot conceive of moral entities or past entities which could constitute the references of the terms of the concerned disputed class. Again, then are some fields where the real issue will be deflected if realism is characterized as entity realism, e.g. realism in mathematics and realism about mental states. This critique has been elaborated by Dummett.[4]

Dummett prefers to say that the disputed class consists of statements, and not of entities or terms. This, he thinks, enables him to overcome the difficulties encountered by entity realism. He characterizes realism as the belief that every statement of the disputed class is either (determinately) true or (determinately) false (i.e. the principle of bivalence applies generally to these statements). Dummett's formulation of realism may be referred to as statement realism or semantic realism.

We see that Dummett quite significantly characterizes realism in terms of the semantic principle that every statement is either true or false. Although in his earlier writings Dummett equates realism with acceptance of bivalence, in his later writings he takes this acceptance of bivalence to be only one of the necessary conditions for realism. Anti-realism is accordingly characterized as the denial of any of the necessary conditions for realism.[5] Since, the principle of bivalence involves the concept of truth, Dummett calls the realism/anti-realism issue a semantic one. The principle of bivalence with respect to a disputed class is a peculiar feature of the classical conception of truth. By "the classical conception of truth" I mean the Tarskian conception of truth of which two remarkable features are: (i) a statement is true by virtue of the things as they are in the world; and (ii) truth is recognition transcendent.

---

[4] Cf. Dummett, 1982, "Realism", and 1978b, "Truth" .

[5] Dummett, 1982, op. cit.

The realist is a propounder of the classical notion of truth. If one is to be a realist concerning a disputed class of statements then one must admit the classical objective truth for the statements of that class. Given a statement *A* of the disputed class, *A* is either true or false only if truth neither depends on our recognition nor on our recognizability. On the other hand, to be an anti-realist one must deny at least a particular feature of the classical notion of truth associated with the principle of bivalence, viz. the feature of recognition transcendence. In other words, he must admit a non-classical conception of truth.

Let us now explain, after Dummett, the interrelation between a semantic theory (or a theory of truth), a theory of meaning and logic. According to him, a semantic theory forms the base of a theory of meaning.[6] What shape would a theory of meaning take depends upon the kind of theory of truth which forms the base of it. So the acceptability of a theory of truth depends upon the acceptability of the theory of meaning of which it forms the base. If a classical notion of truth forms the base of a theory of meaning then the theory of meaning may be called a Classical Truth Conditions Theory of meaning (henceforth CTTM). If a non-classical theory of truth, i.e. a theory of truth which does not capture the classical conception of truth as specified above, forms the base of a theory of meaning then the theory of meaning may be called a classical theory of meaning. It can further be said that if a non-classical theory of truth, where truth is defined in terms of verification/falsification, forms the base of a theory of meaning then the theory of meaning may be called verificationism/ falsificationism. Although from the point of view of constitution the theory of truth leads to the theory of meaning, the acceptability or justification of a theory of truth depends upon the acceptability or justification of the corresponding theory of meaning. Dummett holds that which notion of truth is appropriate for a class of statements depends upon which theory of meaning exploiting a notion of truth explains satisfactorily our understanding of those

[6] Dummett, 1982, op. cit.

statements[7]. Thus we see that acceptance CTTM leads to the acceptance of the classical conception of truth, and so to that of the principle of bivalence. On the other hand, acceptance of verificationism leads to the acceptance of the non-classical conception of truth and so to the denial of the principle of bivalence, i.e. anti-realism. So, Dummett justifies the theory of truth on the basis of the theory of meaning.

Regarding the relation between a semantic theory and logic, on the other hand, Dummett has explicitly stated that acceptance of the semantic principles determines acceptance of the logical laws.[8] Dummett seems to borrow this idea from Frege.[9] He has stated some semantic principles and the corresponding logical laws some of which are given below:

1. Every statement *A* is either true or false — this semantic principle is called the principle of bivalance.

   The corresponding logical law is:

1′. *A* or not *A*, in symbols, $Av\neg\ A$ — this is known as the Law of Excluded Middle.

2. No statement *A* is true nor false — this semantic principle is called by Dummett the principle of *tertium non-datur*.

   The correspondinng logical law is:

2′. It is not the case that neither *A* nor not *A*, in symbols, $(\neg\ \neg\ \ AV\neg 1A)$. This logical law has been called by Dummett the Law of Excluded Third.

We can note first that there is a use/mention difference in the formulation of a logical law and the corresponding semantic principle. In stating logial laws the schematic letter *A* has been used while in stating the semantic principles the schematic letter *A* has been mentioned. However, the important thing in that Dummett contends that acceptance of semantic principles entails

---

[7] See Dummett, 1981, "Realism", pp. 434-35, 446.

[8] Cf. Preface to *Truth and Other Enigmas*.

[9] See Dummett, 1981, op. cit., p. 433.

acceptance of the corresponding logical laws, but not vice versa.[10] In a semantic theory truth may be defined in such a manner that the principle of bivalence holds. If such a semantic theory forms the base of a theory of meaning then the resulting theory of meaning will be CTTM. The logical counterpart, i.e. the logic determined by this semantic theory will include the Law of Excluded Middle. This logic is called the classical logic. Contrariwise, if truth is defined in such a manner that the principle of bivalence does not hold in general, and if such a theory of truth forms the base of a theory of meaning then it is called the non-CTTM. If truth is defined in terms of verification so that the principle of bivalence does not hold in general and such a theory of truth forms the base of a theory of meaning then the resulting theory of meaning is called the verificationist theory of meaning. The corresponding logic does not include the Law of Excluded Middle. The logic resulting from the verificationist theory of meaning is, says Dummett, intuitionistic. The interrelation between the different aspects of Dummett's philosophy of language, as explained above, can be represented through a diagram.[11]

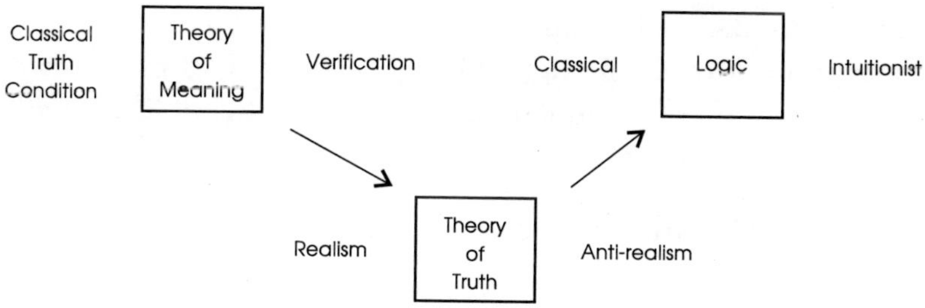

Here "→" designates the order of justification and the visible physical position suggests the order of determination or constitution of the different aspects. Here it is to note that a theory of meaning justifies a theory of truth in the sense that only that theory of truth is acceptable which enables us to construct a right

---

[10] See Preface to *Truth and Other Enigmas.*

[11] Cf. (i) Dummett, 1977, *Elements of Intuitionism,* pp. 370-71; (ii) Preface to *Truth and Other Enigmas,* pp. xxviii-xxix.

theory of meaning. A theory of truth justifies a logic in the sense that only that logic would be accepted if it is grounded in a right theory of truth.

Now we should come back to the original issue — the notion of truth in the theory of meaning as viewed by Dummett. His view about truth in a theory of meaning has got two parts — the negative and the positive. In the negative part we find some major points:

(i) refutation of realism or at least putting realism at stake,

(ii) refutation of the principle of bivalence,

(iii) refutation of the feature of recognition transcendence of the classical conception of truth, and

(iv) refutation of the classical truth conditions theory of meaning.

In the positive part either he replaces truth by verification or he gives a new definition of truth. In the negative part he first proves (iv), then on the basis of it (iii). Here his general thesis is that a semantic theory is justified by the corresponding theory of meaning. Proof of (ii) depends upon the proof of (iii). Here it is presupposed that bivalence is implied only by the classical conception of truth. By definition of realism, (i) is established immediately after the proof of (ii) is given. (iv) is established with the help of a reductio.

The Informal Reductio Proof

Dummett derives a contradiction from the supposition that meaning is truth condition where truth is conceived classically and that we know the meaning of undecidable sentences in the following manner.

First of all, he takes as a premiss, the truth of which will be proved later, that knowledge of truth conditions of sentences is the ability to recognize that the truth conditions have obtained when they have obtained. The second premiss is that meaning consists in truth conditions. Now, if meaning consists in truth conditions and the first premiss is true then to know the meaning of a sentence is to have the ability to recognize that the truth conditions have obtained when they have obtained. In particular, the knowledge of the meaning of an undecidable sentence must also consist in the ability to recognize that the conditions which make it true have obtained when they have obtained. But undecidable sentences are, *ex hypothesi*, such that we cannot recognize that their truth conditions have obtained when they have obtained. This is a fact admitted by the truth condition theorists and so can be admitted as a premiss. So we are to say, on this theory, i.e. the theory that meaning consists in truth conditions, that we do not know the meaning of undecidable sentences. But it is a fact that the meaning of undecidable sentences too are known by us. This too can be treated as a premiss because it is admitted by the truth condition theorist. Thus, we are to say that we know and do not know the meaning of undecidable sentences which is a contradiction in terms. So, meaning does not consist in classical truth conditions.

In this argument the crucial point is that knowledge of truth conditions consists in the ability to recognize that the truth conditions obtain if and when they do. Dummett has established it separately. Let us explain this point in some more detail. Dummett holds not that CTTM cannot be a theory of understanding, i.e. CTTM can account for the knowledge of truth conditions of all sentences. The recalcitrant set is consisted of undecidable sentences. For Dummett a satisfactory theory of meaning is a theory of understanding, i.e. it can account for, among other things, the knowledge of that in which meaning consists of any sentence. But CTTM cannot explain the knowledge of meaning of undecidable sentences. For knowledge may in principle be either explicit or implicit. Knowledge is explicit when the person can state what he knows, i.e. when he can assert some sentences that express the content of his knowledge; and then, of course, it is implied that he knows the meaning of the sentences that he asserts. Dummett thinks that knowledge of truth conditions must be implicit. Since to explain all knowledge of truth conditions as explicit knowledge would necessarily be circular, any such explanation presupposes what it is to know the truth conditions of some sentences. An ascription of implicit knowledge must always be explainable in terms of what counts as a manifestation of that knowledge, viz. the possession of some practical ability. When it is a knowledge of the meaning of a sentence that is in question, the practical capacity which constitutes the knowledge must itself be a linguistic ability. Now, if a person knows implicitly the truth conditions in knowing the meaning of a sentence then the practical ability to which this knowledge is correlated would be the ability to decide that the truth conditions of this sentence have obtained, when they have. The undecidable sentences are such that we can never devise any effective procedure for deciding the truth of them. Since we cannot have any practical ability for deciding whether or not the truth conditions of those sentences have obtained in a particular situation, CTTM fails to be a theory of understanding in the case of undecidable sentences.

It is obvious that this failure on the part of CTTM is a direct consequence of a particular feature of the classical conception of truth, viz. the feature of recognition transcendencce which is associated with the principle of bivalence. So, this particular feature of the classical conception of truth is to be rejected, because for Dummett a semantic theory is justified by the theory of meaning of which it forms the base. Thus (iii) is proved. It has already been shown that the principle of bivalence can be accepted only if this particular feature of the classical conception of truth is admitted. Since this particular feature is rejected by Dummett, consequently the principle of bivalence is also rejected. This establishes (ii). Now, since the principle of bivalence defines realism and bivalence fails, realism is refuted or at least realism has been put at stake by Dummett. So (i) is also established.

Thus, we see that Dummett explains the failure of the principle of bivalence on the basis of the failure of CTTM (i.e. the truth conditions theory of meaning of which the classical conception of truth forms the base). This has been possible for him because he thinks that a semantic theory is justified by the theory of meaning of which it forms the base. Consequently, the Law of Excluded Middle cannot be accepted as a logical law in our natural language, since for Dummett semantics determines logic and the Law of Excluded Middle is the logical law corresponding to the semantic principle of bivalence. Dummett's refutation of realism is extremely important because this refutation in its turn suggests revision in the classical logic.

In his earlier writing[12] the arguments for rejecting bivalence were not made explicit. The arguments have been made explicit in his later writings. One of these arguments has already been put forward. Another argument, very close to the one given above, is that if meaning is given in terms of the classical notion of truth conditions then the obvious fact that meaning is always communicable will be neglected. "An individual cannot communicate what he cannot be observed to communicate."[13] So the meaning of a statement is determined solely by use. But if CTTM is adopted for natural language then meaning and use will be segregated in the case of undecidable sentences. This concludes the negative part of Dummett's view regarding the notion of truth in the theory of meaning.

Before coming to see what Dummett says in the positive part of the view about the notion of truth in the theory of meaning let us now concentrate on what emerges from Dummett's critique in the negative part including the possible ways out and the solution actually given by Dummett. Dummett rejects the particular feature of the classical notion of truth which is associated with the principle of bivalence — the feature of recognition transcendence. The most direct argument he has given for rejecting this feature is that CTTM fails to account for the knowledge of meaning of statements of a kind of the natural language, and so is inadequate. This inadequacy is due to this particular feature of the classical notion of truth. So,

---

[12] Cf. Dummett, 1978b, op. cit., pp. 14-15.

[13] "The Philosophical Basis of Intuitionistic Logic", ibid., p. 216.

he rejects this particular feature of the classical conception of truth. CTTM has got two parts — (i) meaning consists in truth conditions, and (ii) truth is classical. It seems that Dummett rejects (ii) but retains (i). It is impossible for Dummett to deny the obvious fact that a sentence is true iff what the sentence means obtains, i.e. the fact that the meaning of a sentence and the condition the obtaining of which makes the sentence true are identical. To quote him: "The sense of a statement is determined by knowing in what circumstances it is true and in what false."[14] Here by "sense", which he uses interchangeably with "meaning", he means the content of a sentence, or more specifically the content of an assertion. We have already seen that among the different features of the classical notion of truth two are remarkable ones: (a) truth consists in correspondence, and (b) Truth is recognition transcendent. Of these two, the former is for Dummett unobjectionable.[15] He thinks that the Achilles' heel in CTTM is the latter feature of the classical notion of truth, i.e. the feature of recognition transcendence which is associated with the principle of bivalence.

The difficulty in a theory of meaning based on the classical conception of truth arises from the fact that the truth (and truth conditions) of many sentences of our language appears to transcend our powers of recognition. The difficulty can be resolved in at least two different ways. One may retain the concept of truth as it is in the classical thought, i.e. as recognition transcendent but replaces it from the central place in the theory of meaning by some other concept. Another possible way of resolving the difficulty is to retain the central position of the notion of truth (truth conditions specifically) which it has in CTTM but revise the notion of truth as understood classically. It has not been clearly indicated as to which of these two ways has actually been followed by Dummett. There are suggestions in his writings which lead us

---

14 Cf. Dummett, 1978b, op. cit., p. 8

15 "The text describes the principle . . . recognizable circumstances determine it true or false" — postscript of Dummett, 1978b, op. cit., p. 23.

to think that Dummett favours the former alternative. But a large number of Dummettian scholars tend to interpret Dummett as subscribing to the latter view for the reasons discussed above. The reasons are: (i) Dummett does not deny, rather defends, that meaning consists in truth conditions; and (ii) he rejects the classical conception of truth. Let us quote some passages from the different writings of Michael Dummett:

> Realism about a given class of statements . . . is thus a thesis about the appropriate notion of truth for such statements. . . .[16]

Again,

> The solution is to abandon the principle of bivalance. An understanding of a sentence may now be taken to consist in a knowledge of the condition under which a statement has been conclusively established to be true. . . .[17]

The question still remains, on the part of these interpreters, to settle, about the significance of the texts where Dummett categorically dislodges the notion of truth from the central position of a theory of meaning. This problem is resolved in two different manners. Some of these interpreters hold that the texts where Dummett says this represent his earlier view. In his later writings he has changed this view.[18] In his later writings he recognizes that in almost any theory of meaning "we can represent the meaning (sense) of a sentence as given by the conditions for it to be true".[19] The other interpreters contend that these texts only suggest that the classical conception of truth is to be dislodged, not truth simpliciter.

There are at least four possible alternative ways of constructing a theory of meaning:

(i) Where meaning is given by something other than truth

---

16 See Dummett, 1981, "Realism", op. cit., p. 434.

17 Dummett, 1977, op. cit., p. 375.

18 Prawitz, 1987, "Dummett on a 'Theory of Meaning'".

19 Cf. Preface to *Truth and Other Enigmas*, p. xxii.

conditions; (ii) meaning is given in terms of truth conditions, where truth is understood classically and undecidable sentences are included in the set of meaningful sentences; and

(iii) meaning is given in terms of truth conditions where truth is understood classically and undecidable sentences are eliminated from the set of meaningful sentences; and

(iv) meaning is given in terms of truth cconditions, undecidable sentences are not eliminated from the set of meaningful sentences but truth is not understood classically.

Dummett rejects (i) because it is counter-intuitive.[20] The argument for rejecting (ii) has already been given, (iii) is not accepted by him because it goes against the fact that undecidable sentences are meaningful. So, he advocates (iv).

Thus, we see that in the positive part of his view Dummett has retained the central place in his theory of meaning for the notion of truth. So, even for him the core theory is the theory of truth. The role played by the notion of truth in his philosophy of language is very important. Briefly speaking, it makes his theory of meaning (sense) satisfactory,[21] it also makes the construction of a viable theory of force (use) possible although it is not very clear how he proposes to build a theory of force on a theory of meaning. Furthermore, it gives rise to an adequate logic.

Although Dummett has retained the notion of truth in his theory of meaning he has not retained it as it was in CTTM. We can try to comprehend what the notion of truth is like as understood by Dummett.

First of all, truth is not recognizability transcendent. Every statement of which truth can be predicated is recognizable as true, if it is true. The consequence of this feature is that we cannot accept the principle of bivalence, i.e. the principle that every statement is either true or false. Second, this notion of truth does

---

20 See n. 18.

21 See preface to *Truth and Other Enigmas*, p. xxiii.

not allow the possibility of a statement's being neither true nor false. In other words, it admits the principle of *tertium-non datur*, viz. no statement is neither true nor false. In his famous essay "Truth" Dummett has shown that violation of this principle leads to the violation of the equivalence thesis, viz. that a sentence *P* is equivalent with the sentence "It is true that *P*" which he intends to defend because he thinks that if a theory of truth fails to maintain this then it will lead to infinite regress as suggested by Frege.[22] Again it is admitted that a statement is true by virtue of states of affairs.[23] Besides, it is also to be noted that the states of affairs by virtue of which sentences are true are recognizable.

Dummett observes that an intuitionist can develop a theory of truth for the language of mathematics in terms of proof incorporating all of these features. He extends the intuitionist's definitions at truth to the natural language weakening the notion of proof to verification. Dummett has modified the definition of truth through different stages. In his final version he says that an intuitionist can say that a mathematical statement is true iff there exists a proof of it.[24] Here the word "exist" is to be understood intuitionistically.[25] While giving the final version of his definition of truth he says that an intuitionist need not say that a (mathematical) proposition *A* is true iff we have proved *A*. He should rather say that *A* is true iff we are able to prove *A*. If there exists a proof for a statement to the effect that we cannot have a mathematical construction which counts as a proof of it then the

---

22 Cf. preface to *Truth and Other Enigmas*, pp. xx, xxiii, xix.

23 Cf. Dummett, 1978b, op. cit., p. 8 and also see n. 15.

24 Dummett, 1982, op. cit., p. 91; 1977, op. cit., p. 19.

25 For the intuitionist "there exists a proof of a mathematical statement" means that a mathematical construction can be given which counts as a proof of it. To know which mathematical construction counts as a proof of a statement is to know under what condition it is assertable. This is, for the intuitionist, nothing but knowing its meaning. So, for the intuitionist, meaning consists in assertibility conditions or proof conditions. If such a condition obtains or exists (in the intuitionist's sense) then the statement is true and vice versa. Thus, we see that for the intuitionist assertability conditions, proof conditions and truth conditions are the same.

sentence is false. The so-called undecidable$_1$ sentences which we may call undecidable are, for the intuitionists, really false ones. But we know their meanings, because to understand the meaning of a sentence is to know what counts as a proof of it. We have an ability to recognize such a construction for a so-called undecidable sentence. So, for the intuitionist if a sentence is not true, i.e. if we cannot have a mathematical construction which counts as a proof of it, it is tantamount to its being false. So the principle of *tertium non-datur* is preserved. But this notion of truth does not allow the principle of bivalence. Because there are some statements for which we have not yet been able to construct any mathematical construction which counts as a proof of it or under which statements of this kind are assertible. Let us call these sentences undecidable.$_2$ So, we cannot say that these statements are true, neither can we say that they are false. Because uptil now we have failed to prove that we cannot have such a construction. Neither can we assert them, nor can we deny them. So, the principle of bivalence does not hold for them.

In this context let us take an example considered by Niel Tennant.[26] The example taken by Niel Tennant is Goldbach's conjecture, viz. that for every even number n greater than 2, there are prime numbers p, q such that $n = (p + q)$. We know the meaning of this statement. If a construction is proposed for being considered as a proof of this statement, we can determine whether or not it really constitutes a proof of it; we know what counts as a proof of it. A mathematical construction would constitute a proof of this statement if it provides two constructions of primes p, q. Such that their addition is 4 (this is the basis); and provides an effective prodcedure for constructing two primes p, q such that their addition is $2k$, if two constructions of primes p, q are given such that their addition is $2\ (k - 1)$, where $k > 1$. But this statement (Goldbach's conjecture) is undecidable. Neither can we show that such a proof can be constructed nor can we show that it cannot be constructed. By this is not meant that it is impossible to prove

[26] Tennant, 1987, *Anti-Realism and Logic*.

and impossible to refute it. "Undecidable" means that we do not at present possess (an effective method for finding) either a proof or a disproof of it. Goldbach's conjecture, though undecidable$_2$ is meaningful. Since it is undecidable$_2$ the principle of bivalence does not apply to it, but it obeys the principle of *tertium non-datur*, for which the reason is given before.[27]

Thus, we see that Dummett's notion of truth is not epistemic as it is usually supposed to be, because a statement is being true does not depend upon a person's knowledge. A statement may be true even if we do not know it to be true. A statement may be true by the existence of a proof of it, a proof which may not be actually known by us. Note that Dummett does not say that a statement may be true even if we cannot know it to be true. Sometimes Dummett hesitates to define truth in terms of the existence of proof. The reason for his hesitation is that to admit the objective realm of proofs would be a betrayal of the principles that lead us to reject CCTM in favour of a verificationist one, i.e. it would beg the question. Dag Prawitz removes this hesitation by saying that in the objective realm of proofs there can be no question of the existence of a proof that is not in principle recognizable by us.[28] This is so because a proof is by its very nature something that is related to our recognitional capacities, unlike the classical truth conditions that are understood as possible obtaining although we may be in principle unable to recognize what they obtain.

It is evident from the above exposition that even if Dummett is supposed to say that proof (or verification) is the central notion in his theory of meaning he cannot be said to replace the notion of truth by that of proof, because he defines truth in terms of proof (or in terms of the obtaining of proof conditions). Saying that

---

27 It is important to note that in the case of undecidable, the intuitionist can give a proof to the effect that no construction can be given which proves it. But in the case of undecidable, he neither can give such a proof nor can he give a proof to the effect that no construction can be given which disproves it.

28 Prawitz, 1987, op. cit., p. 154.

Dummett replaces truth in his theory by proof is only half of the story. He replaces only classical truth, and not truth simpliciter. So, to say that the central notion in Dummett's theory of meaning is proof or verification in terms of which he defines truth and to say that the central notion in Dummett's theory of meaning is truth, which is verificationist in nature, are two ways of saying the same thing.

Thus, we can say that it is not quite correct to say that Dummett is banishing the notion of truth from the central place in his theory of meaning. Even in his theory of meaning the notion of truth occupies the central place. Dummett's charge against TTM is that here the notion of truth is worngly supposed to be recognition transcendent. Actually the notion of truth is not, says Dummett, recognition transcendent, i.e. the states of affairs, which constitute the content of statements the obtaining of which make them true, is recognizable in principle. Dummett's theory of truth differs from that of Tarski which captures the classical conception of truth to the extent that while Tarski's theory allows the possibility of the states of affairs to be recognition transcendent, Dummett's theory does not.

If we look at the constraints, as admitted by Dummett, which a satisfactory theory of truth must satisfy then we will see that one of them is the equivalence thesis, i.e. for any sentence *S*, *S* is true iff *S*. Now the question about the definition of truth as suggested by Dummett is whether it can satisfy this constraint. The final version of his definition of truth is, for any sentence *S*, *S* is true iff there exists that which counts as a proof (or verification) of *S*. In order to say that this definition satisfies the above constraint we have to admit the equivalence "*S* iff there exists that which counts as a proof (or verification) of *S*". But this equivalence is suspect even if "exist" is understood intuitionistically.[29]

[29] This point was raised by my teacher, Prof. Pranab Kumar Sen, Jadavpur University, while I was discussing with him about the definition of truth as suggested by Dummett.

Notes

I am indebted to Dr Amita Chatterjee without whose constant inspiration it would have been impossible for me to write this paper. She also read the first draft of the paper and made many suggestions which led to its substantial improvement. I read this paper at the Calcutta Logic Circle. I have benefited from the response of the members of the Circle, especially from Dr Ranjan Mukhopadhyay, Dr Mihir Chakraborty and Smt. Rupa Bandyopadhyay.

3

Ayer's Two-Tier Theory of Language

If one asks: Is A.J. Ayer a realist?, it would be instantaneously answered "No, he is not a realist, neither is he an idealist, he is rather a phenomenalist". This instantaneous reply to the above question can have a rationale, but the rationale, although appears to be cogent enough, is not really so. This chapter discusses that he can no longer be said to be a phenomenalist and I shall show this in the background of his two-tier theory of language.

The issue of realism simpliciter is not intelligible to us. It has always to be relativized to a class of statements.[1] One may be a realist concerning material object statements and not a realist concerning moral statements. While I am interested in discussing the issue of realism in the context of Ayer's philosophy, the class of statements I have in mind is constituted by statements concerning physical objects. So, our question is: "Can Ayer legitimately be said to be a realist concerning statements about physical objects?". Again, in raising this question I give a specific sense to the word "realism" — the Dummettian sense.[2] A realistic theory concerning a given class of statements is one which interprets these statements in the classical bivalent semantics. A realist, concerning a given class of statements, admits that each statement of the class is either determinately true or determinately false and in the determination of their truth condition the notion of reference plays an important role. Keeping this sense in mind I shall discuss whether Ayer is a realist or not concerning statements about physical objects.

1 Dummett, 1978, "Realism".

2 Dummett, 1982, "Realism".

Our decision in this regard, however, will follow a detailed analysis of Ayer's view of our understanding of statements concerning physical objects. According to Ayer, we cannot have knowledge of meaning of statements concerning physical objects without having an understanding of statements concerning percepts (sense data). He says:

> . . . any knowledge of the world which anyone acquires is bound to be based upon his own experiences.[3]

He distinguishes two kinds of talks — talk about our experiences and talk about physical objects — and observes that our talk about physical objects depends upon our talk about our experiences. We cannot talk about physical objects directly; we talk about physical objects through our talk about our experiences. Here we see that Ayer perhaps proposes a two-tier theory of language.

Since, for Ayer, we cannot give any sense to the physical object statements without resorting to our understanding of statements concerning our experiences, it is quite natural to suppose that Ayer is advocating a phenomenalist doctrine. But this supposition is false. Let us first be very clear about what the word "phenomenalism" means. Phenomenalism is a form of reductionism. The phenomenalist holds that physical objects are reducible to percepts. All that is meant by this reduction is that statements about physical objects can be completely translated into statements concerning percepts. Anti-realism often takes the form of reductionism. Complete translation of statements of one class into those of another implies that the referring expressions occurring in the statements of the former class do not have a genuine reference, and to their reference have no role to play in the truth determination of the statements of the former class. So, such a thesis turns out to be anti-realistic. The class of statements into which the statements of a given class is reducible may be called the reductive class for the given class of statements. It is quite possible for a reductionist to uphold an anti-realistic view

---

[3] Ayer, 1973, *The Central Questions of Philosophy*, p. 98.

concerning a given class of statements although he takes a realistic attitude towards the reductive class for the given class. A phenomenalist is an anti-realist concerning physical object statements but he may advocate realistic view concerning statements about percepts. If he admits the principle of bivalence for the statements concerning percepts and the classical truth conditional semantics (for) the understanding of the statements then he can be called a realist concerning statements about percepts. But a phenomenalist can deny the principle of bivalence or classical semantics for the statements about percepts, and so characterize himself as an anti-realist.

Our concern, here, is whether Ayer is a phenomenalist or not. To decide this we have to enquire about whether he admits complete translatability of physical object statements into statements about percepts. The complete translatability requirement implies that statements of the reductive class can set out necessary and sufficient conditions for the truth of the statements of the given class. Now for the conditions — stated percepts or the statements concerning percepts to be necessary for the truth of the statements concerning physical objects — it must be the case that the statements about physical objects cannot be true when any of the truth conditions stated by the concerned statements about percepts does not obtain; the conditions can be said to be sufficient only if it is the case that the statements about physical objects could not be false when the conditions stated by the relevant statements about percepts obtain. Ayer is of the opinion that no set of conditions stated by any set of statements about percepts is necessary for the truth of a physical object statement; neither is any set of conditions, stated by a set of statements concerning percepts, sufficient for the truth of any statement about physical object. No finite set of singular statements about sense data, says Ayer, can ever formally entail a statement about a material thing.[4] The reason given by Ayer for this observation is that when we try to reproduce the content of a

---

[4] Ayer, 1958, *The Foundations of Empirical Knowledge*, p. 239.

statement about a material thing by specifying the empirical situations that would furnish us with direct tests of its truth, we find that the number of these possible tests is infinite. If the content of physical object statement is to be represented by a statement about percepts, then the statement about percept must be an infinite disjunction of conjunctions, where each conjunction states a finite set of empirical situations. But when someone makes a physical object statement he does not actually envisage an infinite series of situations. Again, no finite conjunction of empirical situations is necessary for the truth of a physical object statement. Ayer says:

> . . . a visuo-tactual continuant may be represented by an indefinite variety of percepts in an equal variety of contexts, so that if the percepts in question had not occurred, some others would have done as well. . . .[5]

Thus we see that Ayer does not admit that the conditions stated by a finite set of statements about percepts constitute a necessary condition for the truth of a physical object statement. These conditions do not constitute, for Ayer, a sufficient condition for the truth of a physical object statement either. He says in his essay "Phenomenalism"[6] that any description of a particular set of percepts will be bound to leave open at least the logical possibility that the observer is undergoing some illusion. Thus we see that the conditions stated by the statements about percepts constitute neither a necessary nor a sufficient condition for the truth of physical object statements. So, we cannot say that physical object statements are completely translatable into statements about percepts. Failure of translatability prompts Ayer to come out of the boundary of phenomenalism. He says that we must conclude then that the phenomenalist's programme cannot be carried through.

Although talk about physical object cannot be reduced to talk about percepts, says Ayer, there is a close link between the two.

---

5 Ayer, 1973, op. cit., p. 107.

6 Ayer, 1969, *Philosphical Essays*, chap. iv.

Our understanding of physical object statements is parasitic upon our understanding of statements about percepts, and also the determination of the truth of physical object statements is based on the percepts described by the relevant statements about percepts. Thus we see two-way dependence of physical object statements on statements about percepts — (knowledge of) meaning dependence and (knowledge of) truth dependence. In a word, the physical world is our construction out of percepts.

This way of presenting Ayer's view, however, is misleading. One may be naturally tempted to conclude from this that Ayer is taking an idealist stance. But this is wrong. He is rather condemning idealism. Ayer points out that what is wrong with the idealists is that they assume that if one starts with percepts he must also start with a percipient to whom the percepts are exclusively attributed. This assumption of these idealists leads to insurmountable difficulties. One of the difficulties is, if the percipient is just the philosopher, which alone would seem to be warranted, he will be hard put to escape the conclusion reached by the German Idealist, Fichte, that "the world is my idea".[7] This proposition of Fichte describes a view commonly known as solipsism and solipsism is a self-contradictory thesis. Here the philosopher tries to propose a view about the world. In proposing this view he presupposes the existence of other persons besides himself, although he explicitly denies, in his thesis, the existence of anything other than his own ideas.

Unlike Bertrand Russell percepts are not treated by Ayer as private entities. Ayer holds that percepts are universals which can be exemplified in anyone's experience. He appreciates the point made by Wittgenstein[8] that for anything to qualify as a language, it must consist of signs which are employed in accordance with rules. If the statements about percepts are to constitute a language, the percepts which are talked about cannot be private. In learning

---

[7] Ayer, 1973, op. cit., p. 98.

[8] Ayer shares Wittgenstein's hostility to the idea of private language. See Wittgenstein, 1958, *Philosophical Investigations*, sect. 243.

this language we have to know that such and such words stand for such and such percepts, e.g. we learn that the word "red" stands for such and such colour. But in learning this we have to identify the percept designated by the words "red". The problem is how can I be sure that this is the percept the word "red" stands for. In a particular context I have innumerable percepts from which I have to discern the percept referred to by the speaker by the use of the word "red". How is this possible? Here Ayer does not hold like Nelson Goodman[9] that identification of percepts is settled by observer's decree. He admits that the decrees must be subject to some independent checks. One can start with one's personal decree regarding the identification of a certain percept and check one's verdict by associating it with one's wide range of percepts. He can cross-check the decree issued by him through his verdicts regarding all the relevant percepts he experiences. In doing this the observer may find that one verdict concerning the identification of a certain percept comes in conflict with other verdicts. Then he rejects that verdict as false. But if no conflict is found then he goes on treating that percept as an instance of the rule he formulates for using the concerned percept word. Ayer holds that this process of cross-checking the observer's verdicts can be extended to comparing his verdicts with those of other users of the language. As in his own case, the observer rejects those verdicts of him which conflict with the verdicts of other users and the verdicts which tally with the verdicts of other users are sustained. "In the end", says Ayer, "we must simply decide that this is an instance of such and such a word. . . ."[10]

From this it seems that for Ayer the formation of rules of using percept terms starts from the observer's own experiences of percepts and they are confirmed by the assents of native speakers. But I think that the process takes into consideration, from the very outset, the assent and dissent of the native speakers. He forms the rules of using percept words on the basis of the uses

---

[9] Goodman, 1977, *The Structure of Appearance*, p. 134.

[10] Ayer, 1973, op. cit., p. 95.

of the words by the native speakers. His rules are also confirmed as right or wrong by the asset or dissent of native speakers.

However, Ayer admits that the observer's rules of using percept words depend ultimately upon the corroboration of them by the native speakers. This reminds us of Davidson. Davidson[11] too says that the meaning theory of a learner is confirmed by the assent of the native speakers. There are explicit differences between Ayer's view of language and that of Davidson. For Davidson it is the sentence which is the primary unit of meaning. This is obvious because he extends Tarski's theory of truth for sentences of a language to his theory of meaning for that language. Ayer perhaps takes words to be the primary units of meaning. Unlike Davidson, Ayer does not have a *theory of meaning*, in the strict sense of the term. A more fundamental difference between these two philosophers is that no trail of Lockean representationalism is found in Davidson's philosophy as it is found in the philosophy of Ayer. So Davidson need not advocate two-tier theory of language. Still the affinity of Ayer's view with that of Davidson lies in the fact that for Davidson the truth conditions formed by the learner for sentences of language, which actually provides rules for using those sentences, are confirmed by the assent of native speakers. Any resistance from the native speaker shows the vulnerability of a certain rule formed by the learner. The rule can stand only if it coheres with the rules used by the native speakers. Ayer too is of the opinion that our final decision concerning the sanctity of a rule depends upon the native speakers' assent.

The language of percepts is called by Ayer the primitive language. Our language of physical objects, which is termed by Ayer the sophisticated language is built upon this primitive language. Ayer says, "unless the primitive language-game were possible, our more sophisticated language-game could not be played".[12] Thus for Ayer there is a stratification in our language — the language concerning physical objects is understood through

---

[11] Davidson, 1986a, "A Coherence Theory of Truth and Knowledge".

[12] Ayer, 1973, op. cit., p. 95.

our understanding of the language concerning percepts.

After having understood the language of percepts the observer goes on to have an understanding of our language concerning physical objects. This attempt is prompted by the constancy of the world the observer speaks about, i.e. the world of experience. The series of percepts the observer experiences due to the change in his positions is recoverable. A reverse series of the same percepts can be experienced by the observer if he goes back to his earlier positions. Even after a long interval he can get back to the previous percepts. "In this way", says Ayer, "percepts which appear to him successively are to exist simultaneously and to occupy permanent positions in an indefinitely extended three-dimensional visual space."[13] Thus the observer reaches the seat of the constancy of his percepts which he treats as physical object — as objects without depending on our knowledge for their existence. Not only the constancy but also the movements of his percepts are explained by the existence of the physical object.

In explaining this the observer learns to use the sentences which describe the physical objects. These sentences are, for Ayer, categorically different from the sentences describing our percepts. Statements concerning physical objects have the status of theoretical constructs in Ayer's system. The situations, which are attached by the observer to the physical object statements and about the conventional association to those statements of which the observer is confirmed by the assent of the native speaker, are not reached by observation but by imagination.

It would be rash enough to say that since the transition from percepts to physical objects is through imagination, physical objects have no real ontological status in Ayer's system and it is impossible for Ayer to admit any public language concerning physical objects. Ayer's system is better understood as a hypothetico deductive system. On the basis of percepts he constructs hypotheses about physical objects. These hypotheses (sentences about physical

---

13 Ayer, 1973, op. cit., p. 100.

objects), however, entail the statements about percepts. Every observer reaches physical objects as explanation of percepts. So each observer associates physical objects to the singular terms occurring in the physical object statements. The reference to the physical object, however, seems to be blind, not sighted. They are referred to as the source of constancy and coherence found in our percepts. The verification of the statements concerning physical objects are made in Ayer's system in the way in which the verification of hypotheses are made in any hypothetico deductive system. As in any scientific system theoretical entities are not imaginary, rather very much related to the objects of observation and experiment, physical objects are not imaginary objects in Ayer's system. Statements about physical objects are also related to the statements about percepts. Thus for Ayer physical object statements constitute a category different from the category of percept statements, although statements of these two categories are not unrelated. The understanding of physical object statements is possible only through our understanding of statements about percepts; the verification of the physical object statement are made on the basis of statements concerning percepts.

Although physical objects, different from percepts (phenomena), are admitted by Ayer, these objects do not enjoy the status of Kantian things-in-themselves. To quote Ayer: "It is not that physical objects lurk behind a veil which we can never penetrate."[14] The truth of the statements concerning physical objects are recognition transcendent but not recognizability transcendent. Whether a certain physical object statement is true or not, whether the truth condition for such a statement obtains or not can be decided, and it can be decided through our verification of the truth condition of the concerned percept statements. Thus although Ayer holds a realistic position, the kind of Dummettian charge[15] raised against Davidson does not affect Ayer's position.

The above discussion shows that Ayer has a two-tier theory

14 Ayer, 1956, *The Problem of Knowledge*, p. 131.

15 Dummett, 1976, "What Is a Theory of Meaning II".

of language. We start with learning our language concerning percepts and through it we acquire our understanding of the language concerning physical objects. I have also shown that Ayer does not think that statements concerning physical objects are reducible to statements concerning percepts. For Ayer there is a gap between physical objects and percepts. Since he does not accept reductionism, he cannot be said to be a phenomenalist, because reduction is the essence of phenomenalism. Although there is a gap between physical objects and percepts Ayer is against the Kantian view that this gap is unbridgeable. The constancy (recoverability) and coherence of percepts enable us to reach the physical object. Ayer is rather a Humean in the sense that he, like Hume, begins with the constancy of percepts. But these two philosophers differ in the conclusions they derive from this premiss and other premisses peculiar to them. Hume uses the constancy and coherence of percepts as an explanation of our being deceived in believing persistent objects different from percepts, while Ayer uses the constancy and coherence as justification for physical objects which are treated as theoretical entities in Ayer's system. Like Mill, Ayer tends to say that physical objects are permanent possibilities of sensation. Thus we are to say that Ayer holds a realistic view regarding physical objects. We cannot even say that for Ayer percepts are private. Because if Ayer accepts privacy of percepts then his theory of language concerning percepts cannot get rid of the Wittgensteinian charge which I have mentioned above. So, he does not advocate anti-realism concerning the disputed class of statements about physical objects as well as concerning statements about percepts. We can rather call him a mild realist regarding these classes of statements.

4

A Prelude to Pragmatics–Semantics Interface

When a diplomat says 'yes',
he means 'perhaps';
when he says 'perhaps',
he means 'no';
and when he says 'no';
he is no diplomat.

When a lady says 'no';
she means 'perhaps';
when she says 'perhaps';
she means 'yes';
and when she says 'yes';
she is no lady. — *Voltaire*

WHAT Voltaire seems to suggest through this remark is that what is said and what is meant, coded information and its use in communication, do not see to coincide in all cases.

This chapter deals with the demarcation of the study concerning what is said and the study concerning what is meant in linguistic communication as well as with their interconnection, if there be any. The former one is usually known as semantics and the latter, as pragmatics.

Such a discussion necessitates one to start with the Gricean picture. The work of Paul Grice[1] exerts a powerful influence on the way philosophers, linguists and cognitive scientists think about meaning and communication.

---

[1] Grice, 1989, *Studies in the Way of Words.*

With a view to explaining how communication is possible in natural language with respect to a particular sentence ϕ and an utterer *U*, Grice stressed the philosophical importance of separating (i) what ϕ means, (ii) what *U* said on a given occasion by uttering ϕ, and (iii) what *U* meant by uttering ϕ on that occasion.

This threefold distinction can be explained with the help of an example given by Grice himself in "Logic and Conversation".[2] Suppose in a selection committee, professor *A* asks another professor *U*, a professor in philosophy, for an evaluation of his student Mr. *X*. Accordingly *U* utters the sentence "Mr *X* has excellent handwriting and is always very punctual" (ϕ). If this is all that *U* utters, the members of the selection committee are likely to conclude that *U* thinks that Mr *X* is not much good in philosophy. There is no temptation to say that the statement that Mr *X* is not much good (or *U* thinks that Mr *X* is not much good) in philosophy is the statement *U* made in uttering the above sentence. The sentence *U* uttered has a clear linguistic meaning (the truth-condition or the propositional content) based on the meanings of its parts and their syntactical arrangement which is what ϕ means as Grice would say; and it seems quite wrong to say that when *U* uttered ϕ, *U* made the statement that Mr *X* is not much good in philosophy. Note that what *U* said and which statement is made by *U* in uttering a sentence in a certain context are taken here as the same. On the other hand, it seems quite natural to say that in the circumstances, what *U* meant (or part of what *U* meant) by making the statement he in fact made was that Mr *X* is not much good (or that *U* thinks that Mr *X* is not much good) in philosophy. This is something that *U* implied by making the statement he made in this particular context, not something implied either by the sentence uttered or by the statement made by uttering the sentence. I shall explain the difference between the implication of an utterance and the implication of a sentence later on.

---

[2] Grice, 1975 "Logic and Conversation", pp. 41-58.

Thus we see that according to Grice, for giving a complete account of communication, we must distinguish with respect to a sentence ϕ and an utterer *U* — (i) what ϕ means, (ii) what is said when *U* utters ϕ in a certain, context, and (iii) what *U* means when *U* utters ϕ in a certain context. (i) is the propositional content of ϕ which is constituted straightforwardly by the truth conditions of it, if ϕ is an indicative sentence which is associated with the central type of speech act, viz. the act of asserting. In "Utterer's Meaning, Sentence Meaning and Word Meaning"[3] Grice takes two additional sentence types to be conventionally associated with the central type of speech act with which sentences in indicative mood are associated. These are the sentence types in the interrogative and the imperative mood. J. Searle in his "A Taxonomy of Illocutionary Acts"[4] has provided an extensive discussion of how a small number of basic speech act types suffices for a theoretically adequate explanation of all of our utterances. I am not going to discuss it here. All that I want to point out is that Grice admits that, the linguistic meaning of the sentences a speaker uses for the purpose of communication is constituted by the truth condition of the sentence. A dispute may arise among philosophers regarding the nature of this truth condition as, for example, we find it in Davidson–Dummett[5] controversy. Montague's notion of truth condition, which is model-theoretic in nature, is again different from the Davidsonian and the Dummettian notions of truth condition.

An account of linguistic meaning, however, does not suffice for giving a complete account of communication. For this we also need an account of (ii) and (iii), i.e. what is said and what is meant.

What *U* said in uttering ϕ in a certain context is, says Grice in his William James Lectures published in *Studies*, "to be closely related to the conventional meaning of the words (the sentence)

---

3 Grice, 1968, "Utterer's Meaning, Sentence Meaning and Word Meaning".

4 Searle, 1975, "A Taxonomy of Illocutionary Acts".

5 Davidson, 1984, *Inquiries into Truth and Interpretation*; Dummett, 1991, *The Logical Basis of Metaphysics*; Montague 1970, "Universal Grammar".

U has uttered". Although the conventional meaning of the sentence uttered determines what is said in uttering the sentence, it cannot determine it fully. For a full identification of what *U* said on a particular occasion, one has to establish, in addition to the conventional meaning of the sentence uttered, at least the references of the referring expressions (e.g. proper name, demonstratives and indexicals) and the time and place of utterance. Grice seems to say that even this additional part is suggested by the conventional meanings of the subsentential components of the sentence. Perhaps what he intends to say is that the conventional meaning of a word like *I* is a function that takes us from a context of utterance to the semantic value of the word in that context, the semantic value (the reference of *I*) which the word contributes to the proposition expressed by the utterance. On this view, made popular by Kaplan's[6] work on the logic of demonstratives, what is said by an utterance depends not only on the conventional meaning of the words but also on the context of utterance; however, recourse to the context of utterance is guided and controlled by the conventional meaning of the words. The meaning of *I* tells us what to look for in the context of utterance for a complete identification of what is said. Once the context is given, what is said can be automatically decoded. Since what is said is determined by the conventional meaning of the sentence and since the conventional meaning is constituted by truth conditions, what is said is also supposed to consist in truth conditions.

Neat and attractive though it is, this view of the matter is rejected by many philosophers. Francois Recananti,[7] for example, contends that in general, even if we know who is speaking, when, to whom and so forth, the conventional meaning of the words falls short of supplying enough information to exploit this knowledge of the context so as to secure understanding of what

---

6 Kaplan, 1978, "D that" 1989, "Demonstratives"; 1989, "Afterthoughts"; 1990, "Words".

7 Recananti, 1993, *Direct Reference.*

is said. He has explained this with examples and proposed that we should introduce certain pragmatic principles for this purpose in addition to the conventional meaning of words and the knowledge of context. However, I do not see any difficulty in admitting that what is said by uttering a sentence is based on the linguistic or the conventional meaning of the sentence. To explain what *U* means in uttering a sentence in a certain context Grice distinguishes conventional implicature from conversational implicature. Grice holds that in uttering ϕ *U* not only says something, *U* also conventionally implicates something. What Grice means by "conventional implicature" can be explained in terms of the following example. Suppose *U* utters the sentence

1. She is poor but she is honest

   rather than the sentence

2. She is poor and she is honest.

Very likely *U* will be taken to imply that there is some sort of incompatibility between poverty and honesty. For Grice this kind of implication is no part of what *U* says because it does not contribute in any way to the truth conditions of the utterance. By uttering (1), *U* has said only that she is poor and she is honest, and this does not entail that there is any incompatibility between poverty and honesty. The implication in question is called by Grice "conventional implicature". He claims that conventional implicature is determined (at least in part) by the conventions governing the words used. What *U* says and what *U* implicates in uttering ϕ together constitute a part of what *U* means. This part can be called what *U* conventionally means. What *U* means in uttering ϕ has another part which can be called what *U* non-conventionally means. This part is constituted by conversational implicature and non-conversational non-conventional implicature. Grice simply allows (does not elaborate) for the possibility of non-conversational non-conventional implicatures and says that they are generated by aesthetic, social or moral maxims. According to Grice, conversational implications are governed by pragmatic principles. So we reach the following breakdown to what *U* meant.

The pragmatic apparatus, which determines conversational implicatures, contains an overarching principle which Grice calls the cooperative principle:[8]

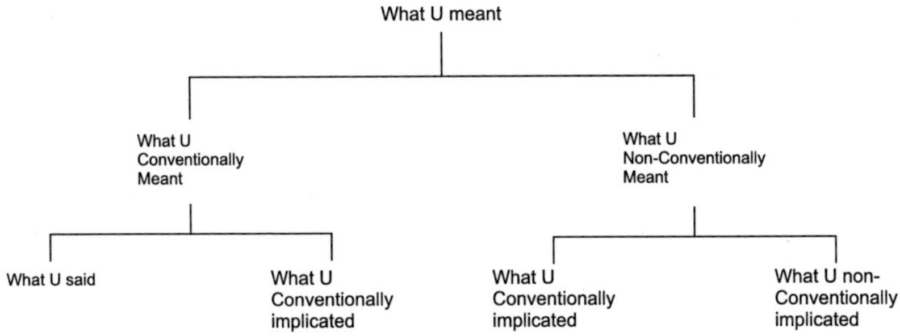

> Make your conversational contribution such as is required, at the stage at which it occurs, by the accepted purpose or direction of the talk exchange in which you are engaged.

Grice distinguishes four categories of more specific maxims and sub-maxims subsumed under this principle, enjoining truthfulness, informativenesses, relevance and clarity.

Quantity: Make your contribution as informative as is required (for the current purposes of exchange). Do not make your contribution more informative than is required.

Quality: Try to make your contribution one that is true. Specifically: (1) do not say what you believe to be false, and (2) do not say that for which you lack adequate evidence.

Relation: Be relevant.

Manner: Be perspicuous, specifically, (1) be brief, (2) be orderly, (3) avoid ambiguity, and (4) avoid obscurity of expression.

Grice's basic idea is that there is a systematic correspondence between what *U* means and the assumptions required in order to preserve the supposition that *U* is observing the cooperative principle and conversational maxims. In the case of professor *U*'s evaluation of Mr *X* if we do not go beyond what is said by *U*, we

[8] Grice, 1975, op. cit.

find an intentional and overt violation of the cooperative principle or of one or more of the maxims. By saying "Mr *X* has excellent handwriting and is always very punctual" (in this particular context) *U* seems at least to have violated one of the maxims of quantity or the maxim of relation. If Mr *X* is one of *U*'s students, *U* must be in a position to volunteer more relevant information than judgements about Mr *X*'s handwriting and timekeeping. Furthermore, *U* knows that more information is required. The hearer is naturally led to the conclusion that *U* is trying to convey something else, something more relevant to the purposes at hand. In the circumstances, if *U* thought that Mr *X* was any good in philosophy he would have said so. So *U* must think that Mr *X* is not good in philosophy and be unwilling to say so. And so *U* has conversationally implicated that Mr *X* is no good in philosophy.

Thus it is evident that what *U* has conversationally implicated could not be communicated to the hearer had the hearer not taken *U* to abide by the pragmatic principles. Mere knowledge of the linguistic meaning of the sentence ϕ uttered by *U* or that of what is said by the speaker in uttering ϕ does not suffice for the hearer to determine what *U* intends to communicate. The hearer's knowledge of the pragmatic principles also plays a significant role in making communication possible. Similarly, the programatic apparatus by itself cannot give a complete account of communication. It has to depend on what is said by *U* in uttering ϕ which is determined by the linguistic meaning of ϕ. So semantics and pragmatics must go hand in hand in giving a complete account of communication. I fully agree with Stephen Neale[9] who says ". . . it is undeniable that the theory of conversation and the theory of meaning are mutually illuminating and supportive." The gap between current semantic theories (together with syntactic theories) and a complete theory of linguistic communication is bridged by pragmatics. Any theory of communication starts with the assumption that when a speaker utters a sentence with a view to communicating something the

---

[9] Neale, 1992, "Paul Grice and the Philosophy of Language".

hearer does understand what the speaker intends to communicate; the task of the theory of communication is to explain how this is possible. I have explained that semantics along with pragmatics can do this job on the basis of a syntactic theory.

One may hold that although the purpose of using language is communication and the task of the philosophy of language is to give an account of communication, semantics is not supposed to do anything with communication. The central task of semantics is to provide a systematic characterization of intuitions concerning truth, falsity, contradiction, entailment and so on. Only linguistic/ conventional meaning is relevant to these things. So semantics need not go beyond the conventional meaning and so it need not depend upon pragmatics. Although this is the view of formal semanticists, the semanticists working on natural language cannot share this view, and here by "semantics" I mean semantics of natural language. Davidson, Dummett and perhaps almost all semanticists of natural language undertake the task of explaining how communication is possible. Dummett in his paper "Language and Communication" ascribes something more to the semantic theory. For him the whole practice of *using* language is to be accounted for by a semantic theory.

The task of semanticists who are trying to extend the technique of formal semantics to natural language becomes easier if recourse to pragmatics is taken. Levinson[10] has rightly observed that pragmatics can effect a radical simplification of the task of semantics.

It becomes easier to explain how pragmatics simplifies the task of semantics if we recall the kind of attack launched by ordinary language philosophers like Strawson[11] against the extension of the device of formal logic to the natural language. These philosophers contend that the semantics of the formal expressions like "&", "v", "$\rightarrow$", "$(\forall x)$" and "$(\exists x)$" cannot capture

[10] Levinson, 1983, *Pragmatics*.

[11] Strawson, 1950, "On Referring"; Strawson, 1952.

the meanings of the natural language expressions "and", "or", "if-then-", "all" and "some": the meanings of the former expressions diverge from those of the latter ones.

Ordinary language philosophers are not alone in claiming to detect these divergences. Positivists and others who belong to the formalist camp recommend in the context of these divergences between formal expressions and their natural language counterparts, the construction of an ideal or logically perfect language.

Grice takes the position that the formalists and informalists (ordinary language philosophers) are mistaken in their common assumption that the formal expressions and the natural language counterparts diverge in meaning. This mistake is due to the fact that each side has paid inadequate attention to the nature and importance of the conditions governing conversation.

Let us take the example of "and". Although it is plausible to suppose that "and" functions semantically just like "&", there are certainly sentences in which it appears to function rather differently.

1. Ann and Bill got married and Ann gave birth to twins.
2. Grice scowled and the student began shaking.

Someone who uttered (1) would typically be taken to imply that Ann and Bill got married before Ann gave birth to twins, and someone who uttered (2) would typically be taken to imply that Grice's scowling contributed in some way to the student's shaking. Thus one might be led to the view that "and" is not always understood as "&", that it is (at least) in three ways ambiguous between truth functional, temporal and causal readings. Grice is sensitive to this point and says that the linguistic (conventional) meaning of "and" is always the same as that of "&", in the case of (1) and (2) "and" has, in addition to this meaning, conversational implicatures which are determined by conversational maxims. The temporal sequence attached to the utterance of (1) can be explained in terms of the fact that each of the two conjuncts describes an event and the presumption that *U* is observing the sub-maxim of manner enjoining orderly deliveries. Similarly the implication of causal connection attaching to utterances of (2) is apparently to be explained in terms of the presumption of the speaker's being relevant.

Since these pragmatic explanations of the different uses of "and" are available, says Grice,[12] we should not allow semantically distinct readings of "and". This remark is supported by Grice's Modified Occam's Razor: "Senses are not to be multiplied beyond necessity". This is how pragmatics helps in preserving the semantics of natural language based on the classical logic.

It can be objected here that simplicity at the semantic level is restored at the cost of introducing pragmatic principles. Grice would reply to this objection by saying that an appeal to the pragmatic principles is not ad hoc, for they are established independently of the semantic concern. He relates these principles to rationality. He holds that any rational activity is governed by these principles. The use of language is one form of rational activity and so it is governed by these principles. Hence it is a good methodological practice to subscribe to Modified Occam's Razor. Thus the task of semantics is simplified by pragmatics.

I have shown how pragmatics simplifies the task of semantics with the help of the logical particle "&". It can also be shown with other logical particles.

Besides bridging the gap between a semantic theory and a complete theory of communication and simplifying a semantic theory the pragmatic apparatus plays a central role in an account of the resolution of ambiguities, the resolution of referential indeterminacy as well as of anaphoric indeterminacy.[13]

So far we have seen that for a complete account of

---

12 Grice, 1989, op. cit.; Grice, 1975b, "Method in Philosophical Psychology".

13 Fillmore, 1981, "Pragmatics and the Description of Discourse"; Wilson and Sperbar, 1981, "On Grice's Theory of Conversation"; 1986, "On Defining Relevance".

communication we need pragmatics as much as we need semantics.

Pragmatics not only bridges the gap between a semantics theory and a complete theory of communication, and simplifies the task of semantics, it also helps in developing a Davidsonian meaning theory for a language. A clear understanding of this statement needs an elaboration of the way in which Davidson resolves the impasse of belief-meaning interlocking in the context of constructing a meaning theory for a language.

Davidson thinks that a meaning theory for a language cannot specify the meaning of every expression belonging to the language in a straightforward manner by entailing a sentence of the form "*x* means *m*" for each expression *x*, because this attempt will lead to many ontological and logical problems. He says that a meaning theory will have done its work if it provides, from a finite base, for every sentence *S* of the class of potentially infinite sentences of the language under study, a matching sentence that gives the meaning of *S*. Davidson points out that a Tarski-type truth theory for a language *L* can adequately do this job, provided the truth theory for *L* is modified in some suitable ways. Tarski's theory of truth provides, from a finite base, each sentence *S* of *L* with a sentence of the form "*x* is true if and only if *p*". This form is called the *T*-schema. Here the variable *x* is to be replaced by the name of some sentence and *p* is to be replaced by a translation of that sentence into the metalanguage in order to obtain the sentence giving the truth condition for the given sentence. This resulting sentence is called the *T*-sentence for the given sentence.

Davidson shows that there is an obvious connection between a definition of truth of the kind Tarski has shown how to construct and the concept of meaning. It is this: the definition works by giving necessary and sufficient conditions for the truth of every sentence, and to give truth conditions is to give the meaning of a sentence. Davidson also points out that to know what the semantic concept of truth for a language is to know what it is for any sentence, belonging to the language, to be true and this amounts to understanding the language.

Although the meaning theory should take the form of a truth theory in Tarski's style, it differs from the truth theory in its intention. The truth theory intends to specify the condition for the truth of every sentence whereas the meaning theory intends to specify meaning for every sentence of a language.

Due to the difference in purpose a truth theory formed in Tarski's style is to be modified to some extent for elevating it to a meaning theory. In a Tarski-type truth theory the notion of synonymy or translation is presupposed. Tarski, however, used this notion in formulating his condition of material adequacy for any truth theory. In a meaning theory one aims at achieving an understanding of meaning as well as of translation by assuming a prior grasp of the concept of truth. It cannot make use of the concept of translation. A meaning theory which uses the concept of translation or synonymy involves a vicious circle and so cannot have any explanatory power. We need to have a meaning theory which would not presuppose the concept of synonymy or that of translation and would yet be such that any T-sentence that was acceptable on the theory would, by virtue of that, could be regarded as yeilding meaning.

For Davidson a meaning theory is nothing but a theory of interpretation. Its task may be seen, says Davidson, as one of redescription. We interpret a bit of linguistic behaviour when we say what a speaker's sentence means on an occasion of use. We know that the expression *Es schneit* has been uttered by a native speaker of German language on a particular occasion to describe a situation and we want to redescribe this uttering as an act of saying that it is snowing. For purposes of interpretation, however, the truth of the *T*-sentence is not enough. A theory of truth will enable us to interpret only if its *T*-sentences state truth conditions in terms of that which can give meaning to the sentences of the object language. So, Davidson's problem is to find constraints on a theory strong enough to guarantee that it can be used for interpretation.

Davidson distinguishes two kinds of constraints — formal

and empirical — on a truth theory so that it can be elevated to the desired meaning theory. The formal constraints follow from the demands that the theory be finitely axiomatized and satisfy the convention *T*. To satisfy these demands the truth theory must rely on something like Tarski's recursive characterization of satisfaction and describe the sentences of the object language in terms of the structure of quantification theory. Davidson says, "the result of applying the formal constraints is, then, to fit the object language as a whole to the procrustean bed of quantification theory".

Besides formal constraints there are empirical constraints too on the truth theory — the conditions under which a *T*-sentence may be accepted as correct. This constraint has a very important role to play in Davidson's meaning theory. In order to elevate the truth theory to a meaning theory for a language the truth theory has to be provided with an evidential basis. It is to be shown that the truth conditions attached by the truth theory to the sentences of the object language under consideration are the truth conditions attached by the native or competent speaker to the respective sentences. The only clue available to us for getting the required evidence, says Davidson, is that the native speaker holds a sentence true in a certain circumstance. But how can we know that such and such truth condition is attached by a native speaker to a certain sentence from the native speaker's holding the sentence true in a certain circumstance? We cannot know this without knowing beforehand what the native speaker believes the situation to be and what his intentions are. The native speaker's holding a sentence true in a certain situation is a function of at least two arguments — belief and meaning. If we could know beforehand what the native speaker believes the situation to be then on the basis of his holding the sentence true we could know the meaning he attaches to the sentence; again if we could know beforehand the meaning the native speaker attaches to the sentence then we could know the belief of the native speaker on the basis of his assent (holding the sentence true). But neither of them can be known independently of the other. Due to this belief–meaning interlocking Davidson concludes that we have to interpret utterance from the scratch, i.e. we have to give radical interpretation to the utterances of the native speaker and in doing this we must somehow deliver simultaneously a theory of belief and a theory of meaning.

The problem then, is this: we suppose that we know what sentences a speaker holds true, and when, and we want to know what he means and believes.

To solve this problem Davidson resorts to the decision theory. A problem similar to the above one in meaning theory is found in the decision theory, choices between gambles are the results of two psychological factors — the relative values the chooser places on the outcomes, and the probability he assigns to the outcomes conditional on his choice. Given the agent's beliefs (his subjective probabilities) it is easy to compute his relative values from his choices; and given his values, we can infer his belief. But given only his choices, how can we work out both his beliefs and his values? The Bayesian decision theory as developed by Frank Ramsey and modified by Jeffrey gives a solution to this problem. Davidson thinks that a similar solution can be given to the problem in the meaning theory, although the solution to the problem in the meaning theory cannot be as neat as the solution to the problem in the decision theory is. Not only the problem in the meaning theory and the solution of it are similar to the problem and the solution of it in the decision theory, Davidson thinks that the meaning theory and the decision theory are complementary to each other, and so he aspires to construct a unified theory of meaning and action.

However, Davidson tries to solve the impasse in meaning theory by appeal to the principle of charity. The interpreter should assume that the native or competent speaker believes the situation to be the same as believed by the interpreter. The interpreter should also project his own logic on to the beliefs of the native speaker, i.e. he should assume that the beliefs of the native or competent speaker form a consistent system. Thus if, on the evidential basis that the native speaker holds the sentences true in a certain circumstance, a consistent set of beliefs can be assigned to the native speaker by an appeal to the principle of charity then thereby we obtain the evidence for truth theory. We thereby put ourselves in a position to know whether the truth theory is correct, i.e. whether the truth conditions specified by the truth theory for the sentences of a language are the truth conditions attached by the native speaker to the sentences in question.

So far we have seen that in providing evidence to a truth theory constructed for a language with a view to elevating the truth theory for the language to a meaning theory of it a Davidsonian has recourse to the principle of charity. Now what is this principle of charity? It is, for Davidson, nothing but a principle of rationality enjoining consistency, truthfulness and other properties. When a learner of a language ascribes a belief concerning the truth condition of a sentence to the native speaker in the context in which the speaker assents to it, it is assumed, by the appeal to the principle of charity, that the native speaker expresses his assent truthfully and consistently with his other beliefs. Now a principle enjoining truthfulness is nothing but one of the pragmatic principles enumerated by Grice. The exposition, given above, of the Gricean pragmatic maxims, shows that the maxim of quality enjoins truthfulness. Thus we see that for the construction of a Davidsonian meaning theory too we recourse to the principle of charity which forms a part of the Gricean pragmatic apparatus. Hence it seems that the construction of a Davidsonian meaning theory for a language is impossible without taking help of pragmatics.

5

Semantic Holism vs. Intentional Realism
An Informational Semanticist's Approach

SEMANTIC holism is a doctrine about the meaning or content of representations — linguistic or mental. So it is a doctrine lying in the theory of meaning, if we are ready to accept the Dummettian distinction between a semantic theory and a theory of meaning. Intentional realism is a doctrine about intentional states. It is a metaphysical doctrine. Fodor has pointed out a conflict between these two doctrines and he sides with intentional realism. He proposes an alternative semantics (anti-holistic) for the intentional states (mental representations) which is within the tradition of informational approaches to content. Fodor has also made an attempt to undermine semantic holism in the sense that the arguments on the basis of which semantic holism has actually been proposed cannot establish it. In this paper I have elaborated Fodor's position in the holism–realism issue and made an attempt to show that the whole project of Fodor is ill-founded.

Let us start with the way in which Fodor shows the conflict between semantic holism and intentional realism. He first formulates holism in Holism: A Shopper's Guide with respect to a property and then specifies semantic holism by applying this formulation of his to a semantic property. He holds that a property may be anatomic or punctate (atomistic). A property is anatomic in the case when anything has it then at least one other thing does, e.g. the property of being a sibling. If x is a sibling then there is at least one other person y who is a sibling. A punctate property is one which might, in principle, be instantiated, by only one thing, e.g. the property of being a rock. An anatomic property is holistic in the sense that if anything of a kind has it then all things of the kind do. The property of being a number is, unlike the property of being a sibling, not only an anatomic property but also a holistic property. If 1 is a number then so is 2 and all other elements of the series. If this notion of holism is applied to the property of having a content then we get semantic holism. The property of having a content is a semantic property. So the doctrine that the property of having a content is holistic, is to say that if anything of a kind has a content then everything of that kind has a content. It is representations which can have content. Representations are of two kinds — linguistic and mental. So there can be two versions of semantic holism. One, if any linguistic representation (i.e. any expression of a language) has content then every linguistic representation (every expression of that language) has a content. Two, if any mental representation (every intentional state of the mind) has a content then every mental representation does have it. Thus, Fodor points out, the issue of semantic holism has given rise to two traditions of thinkers. One tradition stems from the likes of the British empiricists, via such of the pragmatists as Peirce and James, members of the Vienna Circle through the contemporary representatives, such as model theorists, behaviourists and informational semanticists. The second tradition begins from the structuralists in linguistics and possibly the Fregeans in philosophy. Its contemporary representatives include Quine, Davidson, Lewis, Dennett, Block, Putnam, Rorty among philosophers, almost everybody in artificial intelligence (AI) and cognitive psychology.

Fodor draws our attention, first in *Psychosemantics* and then in *A Theory of Content: And Other Essays* and his other writings, to the fact that semantic holism brings forth a major threat to intentional realism. Intentional realism is a metaphysical doctrine about intentional states. Intentional science rests on the realistic understanding of intentional states. In intentional science it is taken for granted that two organisms can be in the same intentional state, i.e. they can have thought tokens which are of the same type. It is assumed here that two persons can have the same belief or desire (which are examples of intentional states). The sharability of the intentional states, which is assumed in intentional sciences, constitute the objective, realistic character of the intentional states. The laws laid down in intentional science achieve generality by quantifying over all the organisms which are in a specified intentional state. These laws take a form such as: "If any organism believes that *p* and desires *q* then it behaves in such a manner". Fodor shows that if semantic holism is true, then the likelihood that intentional science might eventually produce theories whose objectivity and reliability parallel those of the physical and the biological sciences is jeopardized. Thus semantic holism comes in conflict with intentional realism. The conflict between semantic holism and intentional realism is explained by Fodor in the following way.

Let us suppose that *T* is a property which a thought or mental representation has if it expresses a proposition that is the content of some intentional state (say a belief) of mine. Now if *T* is holistic then it might turn out that nobody has a thought that is a token of the same type of which my thought about something is a token unless he also has thoughts which are tokens of the same types of which all my other thoughts are. Because if anybody is to share a thought of mine which has a content (where having a content is supposed to be a holistic property) then he must also be in possession of thoughts having the contents which my other thoughts have. But no two minds ever do share all of their thoughts (intentional states). Hence, if holism is true, no two organisms can be in the same intentional state, i.e. nobody can share any of the thoughts of any other person. Therefore, we have to admit, if holism is true, that the intentional science cannot legitimately make generalizations quantifying over the organisms which are in the same intentional states. No two organisms will ever get subsumed under the same intentional generalization. So, there is no hope for the intentional science which assumes intentional realism. Hence intentional realism is at stake. At this juncture, Fodor holds that we have to choose between semantic holism and intentional realism. One option is to live with semantic holism and look for ways to mitigate the consequences for the intentional science;

another is to stick to intentional realism and do without semantic holism. W.V. Quine, D. Davidson, Stephen Stich, Daniel Dennett, Paul Churchland and others opt for the former, whereas Fodor and other informational semanticists opt for the latter. Fodor proposes an alternative theory of content. He receives the moral from the above conflict between semantic holism and intentional realism that a satisfactory theory of content must be atomistic. His theory of content is within the tradition of informational semantics. In order to retain intentional science, which assumes intentional realism, Fodor specifically gives an informational semantic account of intentional states (mental representations).

Let us recapitulate what has been said so far. I have explained the way in which Fodor first formulates semantic holism and intentional realism, and then shows the conflict between the two. After showing this conflict, he holds that we have two options: either to opt for semantic holism or for intentional realism, we cannot admit both. Fodor opts for the latter and consequently he proposes a theory of content which is not holistic, but is rather atomistic. The theory of content which Fodor proposes falls within the tradition of informational semantics. He has given a detailed exposition of informational semantics in *A Theory of Content and Other Essays* showing how it originates from the Skinnerian semantics discussed in *Verbal Behaviour*, and develops through Dretske's theory in *Knowledge and the Flow of Information*. Finally, he gives his own version of informational semantics. The basic idea of this kind of semantics is that for a representation to have content is to carry information, and the information which constitutes the content is determined solely by the nomic relations between the representation and the extra representational entity. One may pose a methodological query in connection with Fodor's critique of semantic holism. One may call in question the way in which Fodor proposes intentional realism through the rejection of semantic holism. The problem emerges from the second step in Fodor's project, where Fodor holds that there are two options to resolve the conflict. One is to live with semantic holism and the other is to stick to intentional realism. We have seen that Fodor opts for the metaphysical doctrine and he constructs his own theory of content (meaning) which fits his metaphysical doctrine. The reason which he provides for the option he takes is:

> Anti-individualism one may have learned at Mother's knee, but you have to go to Harvard to learn to be a Meaning Holist.
>
> — *Psychosemantics*, p. 60

Although it sounds too emotionally loaded, it does have a solid ground. The ground is that we have a very strong intuition that one organism can share another's intentional states. Now the methodological question can be expressed in this way. In any field, whether it is the field of intentional states or the field of mathematics or any other, we can think of different aspects, e.g. representational, metaphysical, logical and epistemic. In each aspect of every field we have certain intuitions which are supposed to be accommodated in the theory we construct concerning that aspect. The question is: With intuitions of which aspect are we to start our philosophical enquiry? Suppose we are concerned with mathematics. Should we start with building our ontological theory accommodating our intuitions concerning mathematical reality and then construct the other theories concerning the other aspects accordingly? Or should we start with building our theory of meaning accommodating our intuitions concerning the use of mathematical statements and then construct the other theories concerning the other aspects accordingly? We find in our discussion of Fodor's project that Fodor starts with our intuition concerning the metaphysical aspects of intentional states. It is on the basis of these intuitions that Fodor opts for intentional realism and constructs his theory of content of the language of thought. So Fodor seems to suggest that we should settle our metaphysical issues first of all and then proceed for settling meaning theoretic issues. Michael Dummett, on the other hand, gives a diametrically opposite suggestion. In *The Logical Basis of Metaphysics*, Dummett explicitly observes that meaning-theoretic problems should be settled first, and then we can proceed to settle the metaphysical issues via the solutions of the semantic or truth-theoretic issues. He holds that if we are to climb on the metaphysical peaks then we have to start from our base camp of meaning theory. So if Fodor's approach to settle philosophical issues is called the top–down approach Dummett's approach is to be called the bottom–up approach. Davidson's approach comes very close to that of Dummett. Quine seems to say that the base camp is constituted by naturalized epistemology. Thus we are really baffled. Which path should we take? One may hold that we should not give primacy to any of the different kinds of intuitions mentioned above. In our philosophical enquiry, we must go on philosophizing across the board. But this will make philosophical enquiry much more unsystematic than it actually is. At this point, I am sympathetic to Dummett's approach, because the argument given by him in favour of his approach is not very weak. Dummett holds, to repeat, that we should start with building our philosophy of language. The advantage of philosophy of language is that here we do have a definite means of justifying our theory of meaning. Because a satisfactory theory of meaning has to satisfy certain unanimous constraints with the help of which we can check whether or not our theory of meaning is a correct theory. But in the case of metaphysical issues, there is no such means. So our metaphysical theories are to be judged in the light of our theory of meaning. Now if this is granted, then Fodor's whole project appears to be misdirected. The point which I would like to highlight is that Fodor's project is ill-founded. The whole project depends on the conflict he has attempted to show between semantic holism and intentional realism. But it can be pointed out that the argument of Fodor on which he tries to highlight the conflict is not convincing enough. Fodor's argument for this conflict can be schematically stated in the following way:

Premiss 1: Semantic holism is the doctrine that the property of having a content is such that if anything of a kind has it then everything of the kind has it.

Premiss 2: If any intentional state of a mind has a content then every intentional state of the mind has a content [this is a special case of premiss 1].

Premiss 3: Nobody can have all the intentional states of any other person.

From Premisses 1 and 2 we get:

If *A* is to have an intentional state of *B* then *A* must have all other intentional states of *B* having the content they have. From this and premiss 3 we get: Nobody can share any thought of any other person. This conclusion evidently conflicts with intentional realism which is the doctrine that intentional states are sharable. Here it may be argued that premiss 1 presents a very unusual characterization of semantic holism. The question is not really whether anything's having a content depends upon all other things' having a content or not. The real question is whether the content of anything of a kind is determined by the content of all other things of the kind. It is conceivable that all things of a kind have content, one thing's having a content depends upon other things' having content, although it is not the case that the content of anything of the kind is determined by the content of all things of the kind. It is this sense in which philosophers usually use the expression "semantic holism". Semantic holism, with respect to a language, is understood to be a doctrine that the meaning of a sentence is determined by the meanings of all the sentences of the concerned language. But this property of being determined by the contents of other things of the kind is neither explicitly maintained nor is it implied in Fodor's characterization of semantic holism. It can further be said that if the dependence of the very being of the content of a representation on the content of other representations is not mentioned in the characterization of semantic holism then it does not necessarily follow from premisses 1 and 2 that if *A* is to have an intentional state of *B* then *A* must have all other intentional states of *B*. We have seen that Fodor's project of establishing intentional realism through the rejection of semantic holism is based on the supposed conflict between semantic holism and intentional realism. So the success of Fodor's project depends upon the success of showing that the conflict really exists. But I have argued that Fodor fails to show that this conflict really exists. Therefore, Fodor's whole project seems to be ill-founded.

6

Reflections on the Problem of Justifying Deduction

This chapter is a homage to Prof. Pranab Kumar Sen, my revered teacher, whose exemplary style of analysis and enviable clarity and precision in thought and speech have aroused my interest and capabilities in philosophical pursuit. The problem of justifying deduction occupied the core of his research area in philosophy. His interest in this problem emerged from his interest in the problem of entailment on which he concentrated in the early period of his philosophical investigation. I intend to show that his enquiry in this area has far-reaching implications. Although the problem of justifying deduction is a perennial one, Michael Dummett has revived the problem recently with an elegant formulation of it and a critical analysis of the available alternative solutions to the problem along with his own solution to it. Sen was not only well aware of these alternative solutions, he also suggested a new solution to the problem. My own observation here regarding the problem of justification will be preceded by a brief sketch of the alternative solutions to the problem formulated by Dummett including that of Sen.

Formulation of the Problem[1]

Let us begin with the Dummettian formulation of the problem of justifying deduction. Dummett points out that the problem arises at three levels. We can raise the problem at the level of a particular deductive argument. We can ask whether a particular deductive argument is valid or not. We can justify the validity

[1] The problem of justifying deduction is formulated here within a system of natural deduction only.

of the particular argument by deriving the conclusion of the particular argument from its premises with the help of some rules of inference. Here the validity of the rules of inference by which we derive the conclusion of the given argument is assumed. So the question of validity arises again at the level of rules of inference. Here we can ask whether a particular rule is valid or not. We can justify the validity of a particular rule of inference on the basis of the validity of more fundamental or basic rules of inference. But the question of validity arises even at this level of more basic rules. This is the third level at which the question of justifying deduction arises.[2] So, the first level enquiry relates to a particular deductive argument, the second level enquiry relates to a particular rule of inference and the third level enquiry relates to a more basic rule of inference. It is to be noted here that in certain cases of deductive arguments we need not go beyond the second level enquiry.

Alternative Solutions to the Problem

PROOF-THEORETIC JUSTIFICATION

In this kind of justification the validity of any deductive argument or a rule of inference is justified in terms of some purely syntactic rules. So at all levels of proof-theoretic justification of deduction, the justification is given in terms of some rule or other. This, however, supplies only a relative justification. At any level this kind of justification assumes that certain other laws are valid. We cannot have a proof theory unless we have assumed the validity of some rules of proof. The very attempt to give absolute proof-theoretic justification involves either infinite regress or circularity: to give an absolute justification of the validity of a deductive argument, either we have to give justification of the validity of rules of inference of infinite numbers or we have to go round a

---

[2] In his earlier writing Dummett related the problem of justifying deduction at the third level to the utility of deduction. But it was not at all clear, even to Dummett himself, what this third-level enquiry consisted in. In his later writings Dummett relates this third-level enquiry to basic rules of inference.

circle of justification of the validity of rules of inference.[3]

SEMANTICAL JUSTIFICATION

Here the validity of a particular deductive argument is justified in terms of some rules whose validity is justified in terms of some more basic logical laws, but the validity of these more basic laws is not justified in this manner. The justification of the validity of these more basic laws is given through semantical considerations of the logical constants involved in these laws. Modus Ponendo Ponens is such a law. This law involves only the logical constant "→". An argument can be given proving that Modus Ponendo Ponens is valid from the premise which consists in stating that such and such are the semantical properties of the logical constant "→". But this kind of justification inevitably involves a circularity. Because in the very argument showing the validity of Modus Ponens, one inferential step has been taken with the help of this rule.[4] Dummett calls this kind of circularity as "pragmatic circularity".[5] Sen has called it "rule circularity".[6] Sen also argues that the semantical justification involves premiss circularity as well: in the argument proving the validiy of a fundamental logical law, a premiss claims the validity of the logical law itself.[7] Incidentally, Ranjan Mukhopadhyay has argued that this argument of Sen is illegitimate.[8]

However, the question remains whether the alleged pragmatic circularity really vitiates the argument providing semantical

---

[3] A detailed account of infinite regress or circularity is available in (a) Dummett, 1991, *The Logical Basis of Metaphysics*.

(b) Sen, 1991b, *Reference and Truth*.

[4] This point has been elaborated by Ranjan Mukhopadhyay in his doctoral dissertation at Jadavpur University, India and also by Susan Haack, 1976, *Mind*, vol. 85, and Susan Haack, 1982, *Mind*, vol. 91.

[5] See Dummett, 1991, op. cit., p. 202.

[6] See Sen, 1991a, "On the Problem of Justifying Deduction", p. 168.

[7] See ibid.

[8] See Mukhopadhyay, 2000, "Individual Deduction, Rule of Inference and Validity".

justification of the fundamental logical laws. In one of his earlier writings[9] Dummett observes that the answer to this question depends upon the purpose for which the justification is given. If the argument is suasive, i.e. if the argument is addressed to someone who genuinely doubts the validity of the rule of inference, then the pragmatic circularity vitiates the argument. But if the justification is explanatory, i.e. if it is addressed to someone who does not doubt the validity of the rule seriously, but only seeks an explanation of it, then the pragmatic circularity does not make any harm to the argument. As Dummett is concerned with the genuine dispute over the logical laws he dissociates himself from the semantical justification of deductive arguments. He has made this point clear in his later writting:

> In the presence of a genuine dispute over the validity of a logical law, by contrast, pragmatic circularity has to be avoided.[10]

Proof Theorist's Reply to the Charge of Infinite Regress or Circularity

For the purpose of avoiding the charge of infinite regress or circularity proof theorists treat some logical laws (the fundamental logical laws) as stipulated outright initially, without the need of any further justification, to serve as a base for proof theoretic justification of other laws. This subset of logical laws is stipulated arbitrarily. The logical laws belonging to this subset need no further justification. They are treated as self-justifying. So for justifying the validity of a particular argument we need not assume the validity of rules of infinite numbers, neither do we need to go round a circle of justification of rules of inference. Thus it seems that the charge of infinite regress or circularity can be avoided.

The thesis that any set of fundamental logical laws can be stipulated by fiat as self-justifying laws is known as logical formalism. Arthur Prior has brought a strong objection to logical formalism. Introducing the logical constant "tonk" he has shown

---

[9] See Dummett, 1978a, "The Justification of Deduction".

[10] See Dummett, 1991, op. cit., p. 203.

that any statement can be derived from any other statement.[11] So the need of some sort of check is felt at the level of self-justifying rules. It is well known that Nuel Belnap and Dummett have made significant contribution in formulating the kind of restrictions to be imposed on the self-justifying rules. Before coming to these restrictions let us see what Dummett's own solution to the problem of justifying deduction is.

Justification of Dummett

Dummett's solution to the problem of justifying deduction is different from the purely proof-theoretic approach and also from the semantical approach as explained above. A common feature of justifications of deduction of these three kinds is that in the first level the validity of particular arguments is justified by appeal to rules; in the second level the validity of rules is justified by appeal to some basic rules. The difference between these three kinds of justification of deduction arises only in the third level. In proof-theoretic justification the basic rules are stipulated by fiat, like the rules of a game, without any consideration of meaning. In semantical justification of the above kind the validity of the basic logical laws is derived from the meanings of the logical constants involved in these laws. In the Dummettian justification the basic logical laws are treated as self-justifying. Here the validity of the basic laws is not derived from the meanings of the logical constants involved in these logical laws. So the Dummettian justification has affinity to the proof-theoretic justification as in both of these justifications the basic logical laws are treated as self-justifying. But Dummett's justification differs from the proof-theoretic justification as well. The difference is that in proof-theoretic justification the basic logical laws are treated as self-justifying without any consideration of meaning, whereas in the Dummettian justification the basic laws are treated as self-justifying because they are meaning-giving rules. For Dummett being self-justifying and being meaning-giving are not separate things. The basic logical

[11] See Prior, 1960, "The Run About Inference Ticket".

laws, according to Dummett, give meaning to the logical constants involved in the logical laws.

Belnap and Dummett have imposed on the basic logical laws certain restrictions to elevate them to the status of self-justifying or meaning-giving rules of inference. These restrictions help to avoid the unwanted consequences pointed out by Prior. The restrictions given by Belnap are conservative extension and uniqeness. The conditions added by Dummett to this list are harmony and stability.

Hence Dummett admits three levels of justification. The basic logical laws are treated by him as self-justifying in the sense of meaning-giving rules of inference.

Sen's Justification

Sen does not admit three levels of justification of deductive arguments. He observes that the problem of circularity crops up from the idea of three-level justification. So he replaces it by the idea of justifying the validity of particular deductive arguments directly by the basic laws (introduction or elimination rules). The basic laws of logic express the semantic properties or meaning of the logical constants involved in the laws. According to Sen, the justification of the validity of a particular deductive argument proceeds by considering the semantic properties (the meaning) of only the logical constants that occur in the argument.

One possible objection to Sen's justification is that the direct justification of particular arguments is impossible. Let us call the argument which justifies the validity of a particular deductive argument by considering the semantical properties of the logical constants involved in the argument *T*. When *J* considers the semantical properties of the concerned logical constants, what is first of all established is a generality — the validity of a rule. Then the validity of the particular argument is established by showing that the conclusion of the particular argument is inferred from its premisses in accordance with this rule or that the particular argument is an instance of the rule. So the so-called direct justification of particular deductive arguments surrepititiously involves an intermediary justification. Ranjan Mukhopadhyay has raised an objection of this kind against Sen's way of justifying deductive arguments.[12] I think that Mukhopadhyay is absolutely right in raising this objection under one possible interpretation of Sen's way of justifying deductive arguments.

But I think that there is another possible interpretation of Sen's way of justifying deductive arguments. Under this interpretation *J* establishes the validity of a particular deductive argument simply by showing that the conclusion of the argument is derived from its premisses in accordance with certain basic rules which are self-justifying or meaning-giving. Under this interpretation no intermediary justification is involved. Sen perhaps had this interpretation in his mind not the former one, because he treats semantical properties as rules and rules are treated by him as self-justifying. To distinguish his position from that of proof-theorists, Sen says:

> The rules of this kind I propose to call semantically animated rules. The rules in terms of which the conventional derivational justification is given do not have any semantcial life.[13]

Mukhopadhyay might say that in deriving the conclusion of *J*, viz. that the truth conditions of the premises of a particular argument is included in the truth conditions of the conclusion of it, from the premiss of *J*, i.e. the rules which give meaning to the relevant logical constants, we first establish that the truth conditions of any formula of the form of the premisses of the particular argument are included in the truth conditions of any formula of the form of the conclusion of the argument.

Taking the argument

The Tajmahal is beautiful

The Tajmahal is a tourist attraction

---

12 See Mukhopadhyay, 2000, op. cit.

13 See Sen, 1991b, op. cit., p. 187.

∴ The Tajmahal is beautiful and is a tourist attraction

he says that *J* proceeds to show the following: given the semantical properties of the logical constant "&", for any formula *A* and *B*, if *T* is a condition under which both *A* and *B* are true then *T* is a condition under which *A* & *B* are true. This is, says Mukhopadhyay, a general claim, stronger than what is required for justifying only a particular argument.

Here Sen would have replied that *J* need not establish this generality, because this generality is precisely what constitutes the rule which gives meaning to the logical constant "&" from which *J* derives the validity of the above particular argument. So *J* need not establish anything beyond that the particular argument accords the rule.

Mukhopadhyay might again argue that his objection is based on Sen's unusual understanding of rules as mere codifications of how particular arguments are justified by semantical means and so his argument continues to retain its force as long as Sen sticks to this unusual understanding of rules.

I think that this worry of Mukhopadhyay generates from the supposition that when Sen views rules as codifications of how particular arguments are justified by semantical means, he rules out the possibility of deriving the validity of particular arguments from rules. But this supposition is perhaps wrong. Because in the same paragraph in which Sen makes the alleged statement about rules, he distinguishes his way of deriving the validity of particular arguments from rules of inference from the semantical justification as mentioned above.[14] Furthermore, Sen's making of this statement about rules is not essential to what he says about justifying deduction.

So, Sen's way of justifying deductive arguments comes close to that of Dummett. The only difference is that according to Dummett, the validity of particular arguments is justified by rules. The validity of these rules is again justified by some basic rules

---

[14] See Sen 1991b, op. cit.

which are treated as self-justifying or meaning-giving. According to Sen, the validity of particular arguments is derived directly from the basic rules which are treated by him as self-justifying or meaning-giving.

One may hold that the Dummettian justification seems to be preferable to that of Sen, because unlike the semantical justification it is not affected by the charge of circularity. Sen's justification is also sacrosanct so far as the charge of circularity is concerned. But there are certain particular deductive arguments the validity of which perhaps cannot be justified solely with the help of some basic rules of inference. In these cases we have to assume the validity of some non-basic rules and so for the purpose of giving a general pattern of justification we have to admit the Dummettian way of justifying deductive arguments. But this preference seems to be ill-founded, because a Gentzen-style natural deduction system might show the redundancy of non-basic rules. Rather Sen's approach should be preferred for the sake of simplicity.

I am not very seriously concerned, however, with the question of which of these two ways of justifying deductive arguments is correct. Here I want to make a more serious point. The point is elaborated in the following way.

So far we have seen that the right way of justifying deductive arguments rests ultimately on admitting some basic rules of inference which are self-justifying or meaning-giving rules. We have also seen that these basic rules are constrained by certain conditions in order to be self-justifying or meaning-giving rules. We have also seen that these basic rules are constrained by certain conditions in order to be self-justifying or meaning-giving. Here one may think that the enquiry concerning justification of deductive argument has come to an end. But it may be wrong to think so. The legitimacy of the conclusion of the above prolonged enquiry concerning justification of deduction depends upon the solution of another deep philosophical problem to which this conclusion leads.

To have a hunch of this remark we must have a relook at the

self-justifying rules of inference wherein the solution to the problem of justification is found. These rules are meaning-giving rules. A very important question which arises at this point is: What kind of meaning is given to the logical constants by these rules? Sen has said that each row in a truth-table of a logical constant can be treated as a rule-giving meaning to that constant. So the kind of meaning self-justifying rule gives to a logical constant is nothing but the truth-table meaning of it. Dummett cannot admit that a self-justifying rule gives this kind of meaning to a logical constant. Because the notion of truth involved in the truth-table of the kind Sen speaks of is bivalent truth and Dummet, with his anti-realistic stance, is always against this notion of truth. So, until we settle this question we cannot have a grasp of the solution to the problem of justifying deductions. A much more deep philosophical issue which the above solution to the problem of justifying deduction leads to is the issue of a correct theory of meaning. It is said that self-justifying rules must satisfy certain conditions in order to be meaning-giving. These conditions are conservative extension, uniqueness, etc. If we look at these conditions deeply then we will find that they are typical features of an atomistic/molecular theory of meaning. In a holistic theory of meaning conservative extension cannot be maintained. In a holistic theory the whole range of meaning of a language changes with the introduction of new meaning in the language. Similarly the other conditions imposed on the self-justifying rules cannot be maintained in a holitic theory of meaning. So until we decide which of the two competing theories of meaning — atomistic molecular and holistic — is the correct theory of meaning, we cannot succeed in giving a solution to the problem of justifying deduction.

7

The Computational Theory of Mind*

What Is Cognitive Science?

THE computational theory of mind, the most important of the current theories of mind, is advocated by cognitive scientists: Cognivite science officially starts with A.M. Turing ("Computing Machinery and Intelligence", *Mind*, LIX (236), 1950). We had found grand success of physics at the time of Turing, but no successful scientific theory concerning human intelligent or cognitive behaviour could be found till that time. We say that people are exhibiting intelligent/cognitive behaviour when they choose courses of action that are relevant to achieving their goals, when they reply coherently and appropriately to questions that are put to them, when they solve problems of lesser or greater difficulty, or when they create or design something useful or beautiful or novel, etc. Any attempt to give explanation of these activities failed all the way. On the one hand, there was folk psychology, aiming at an explanation of these activities, resorting to common-sense intentionalistic idioms like belief and desire, but it could not acquire the status of a science. On the other hand, there were physics, neurophysiology and like sciences, aiming at giving explanation of these activities, with their purely extensional vocabulary and so they could not get hold of the black box behind these activities. Searle has called this crisis ". . . a remarkable lacuna in twentieth-century intellectual life".[1] At this critical juncture Turing came forward with his cognitive science proposal with a view to

---

* This paper constitutes a part of the findings of my minor research projcet "Turing's Cognitive Model of Logic, Language and Mathematics", funded by UGC.

[1] Scarle, 1988, "*Minds and Brains without Programs*".

removing this lacuna. At present cognitive science is thought to be the most suitable candidate for the removal of this lacuna.

The kind of explanation given by cognitive science is claimed to be on the one hand, unlike folk psychology, a scientific one and on the other hand, unlike physical or neurophysiological models, not purely extensional. Cognitive science views human mind as a computational device. Here all human intelligent/cognitive activities are accounted for in terms of a common set of underlying (internal) processes that are scientifically representable although they are neither physical nor neurophysiological. These underlying mental processes are called by cognitive scientists "computational processes". So their theory of mind is called "the computational theory of mind". Cognitive scientists claim that the underlying computational processes that determine human intelligent activities are the same as those present in computers determining the activities of computers.

Today it is quite common to attribute intelligence (cognition) to both biological (human) and physical (non-human) systems and, in particular, to programmed computers. Intelligence is judged nowdays in terms of the ability to perform intelligent/cognitive behaviour. In 1950 Turing predicted this common use of "intelligence" (or "thinking"). Turing's conjecture was:

> . . . I believe that at the end of the century the use of words and general educated opinion will have altered so much that one will be able to speak of machines thinking without expecting to be contradicted.[2]

This prediction of Turing was based on his celebrated idea of imitation game. The imitation game essentially consists of three players: (a) a computer responds, using a teletype, to various inputs it receives; (b) a human being also responds via a teletype; and (c) a second human being interrogates the other two players providing them with inputs (questions). The object of the game is to see if the second human being can, by asking

---

[2] Turing, 1950, "Computing Machinery and Intelligence".

questions and examining the answers, tell which of the unseen devices is a human and which is a machine. If he fails to do this then the computer can legitimately be said to have intelligence or thinking or cognition. This is commonly known as the Turing test. Turing was confident that digital computers, which are realizations of the universal Turing machine, would be able to befool the human questioner and so could rightly be said to have intelligence.

Allen Newell, Herbert A. Simon, Zenon W. Pylyshyn, Craig A. Kaplan, Jerry A. Fodor and others were deeply influenced by Turing's idea and developed a full-fledged discipline called "cognitive science", which, according to Simon and Kaplan, is the "the study of intelligence and its computational processes in humans (and animals), in computers and in the abstract".[3] Pylyshyn defines cognitive science as "the study of the natural domain of cognition, where cognition includes prototypical phenomena of perception, problem solving, reasoning, learning, memory and so on".[4]

The Computational Theory of Mind

The theory of mind, developed by cognitive scientists, is called "the computational theory of mind". Although cognitive science studies intelligent/cognitive behaviour of humans and computers, any theory of intelligent/cognitive behaviour of humans and computers cannot be said to be the computational theory of mind. One may study the intelligent behaviour of humans and computers with a view to establishing that any such human behaviour can be simulated (produced) in a computer. It is claimed here that as the human behaviour that is called "intelligent" can be simulated in a computer, human mind and computer are equivalent. Pylyshyn calls this kind of equivalence "weak equivalence", because it is with respect to input/output. We can distinguish three aspects of an intelligent behaviour — (a) an input, (b) an output, and (c) an underlying process which

---

3 Simon and Kaplan, 1996, "Foundations of Cognitive Science", p. 2.

4 Pylyshyn, 1996, "Computing in Congnitive Science", p. 85.

correlates (a) to (b). In a study of intelligent behaviour of humans and computers with a claim of weak equivalence all that is claimed is that given any input of an intelligent human behaviour to a computer, the computer will be able to correlate it to the output to which a human being correlates it.

In the computational theory of mind advocated by a cognitive scientist the equivalence claim between a human mind and a computer is, unlike the claim in the study of intelligent behaviour of humans and computers mentioned above, a strong equivalence claim. Cognitive scientists not only claim that the correlation established between an input and an output of an intelligent behaviour by a computer is the same as that established by a human being, but also that the underlying process by which a computer establishes the correlation is the same as that by which a human being establishes it. It is for this strong equivalence claim that philosophers have been interested in the computational theory of mind. I quote here a long passage from an article of Pylyshyn, a famous cognitive scientist, which, I think, is extremely important for having an exact grasp of the computational theory of mind advocated by cognitive scientists. Pylyshyn says:

> The possibility of imitating life by artefact has intrigued people throughout history. But only in the second half of this century has the possiblity of using the special type of artefact that we call a computer been considered seriously as a means of understanding mental phenomena. What is different about this latest interest is that the focus is not primarily on the imitation of the movements (as was the case with early clock-work machanisms) but on the imitation of certain unobservable internal processes. This notion only became conceivable with the gradual emergence, in several disparate areas of intellectual development, of a certain way of understanding mechanisms. This new and more abstract notion of mechanism is entirely divorced from the old-style "mechanical" considerations (such as those that preoccupied Descartes and that Chomsky has characterized as contact mechanics) and is concerned only with abstractly defined operations such as storing, retrieving and

altering tokens of symbolic codes.[5]

Thus cognitive scientists posit a set of abstract computational processes which are, they hold, realized in humans as well as in computers. According to them, these internal computational processes determine all intelligent/cognitive activities of humans and computers. So they have developed a theory of computational process realized in humans and computers, which they think can explain away the mystery of human cognitive behaviour.[6]

Different disciplines have made contributions to cognitive scientists' theory of computational processes realized in humans and computers. Philosophy, for example, has immensely contributed to this theory in two ways — (a) by providing a rigorous method, and (b) by addressing the age-old questions like the question of the nature of human mind and intelligence. Formal logic, a branch of philosophy, has shown how inference processes can be viewed as symbol manipulation and thereby provided some of the foundational ideas for the computational theory of mind. Psychology, like philosophy, has made enormous contribution to this theory. Psychology is a conglomeration of various specialization, each of which has brought its particular contribution to this theory. Psychometry has brought its measures of intelligence and the components of it. Neurophysiology has brought knowledge of the biological structures that support cognition. Experimental psychology has brought a host of information about the speed and limitations of sensory, motor and memory processes. Another discipline that has made sufficient contribution to this theory is Artificial Intelligence (AI). AI has

---

[5] Pylyshyn, 1996, op. cit., p. 53.

[6] Cognitive scientists do not claim to give explanation of all kinds of human behaviour. They aim at giving an explanation of human cognitive behaviour only, although they do not rule out completely the possibility of giving an explanation of other kinds of behaviour with certain modification of their computational theory of mind. For a detailed account of this possibility see D.E. Rumelhart and J.L. McClelland, and the PDP Research Group: *Parallel Distributive Processing*, The MIT Press, 1986, besides Pylyshyn's 'Computing in Cognitive Science'.

provided list-processing languages that permit the modelling of elaborate associative structures — schemes, scripts, frames — to simulate important properties of human semantic memory.[7] AI research has also adapted programming languages built up from so-called productions as a sophisticated interpretation and augmentation of classical stimulus–response relations and stimulus–recognition processes.[8] Linguistics, more specifically psycholinguistics, too have made enough contribution to the computational theory of mind. Psycholinguists have given important suggestions regarding the internal processes working behind our linguistic behaviour.

The System of Computational Processes

Computational processes that determine intelligent/cognitive behaviour in humans and computers function, according to cognitive scientists, in a fixed system of mechanisms, which is called by them the "architecture of mind or cognition". Cognitive scientists are not unanimous as to the nature of this architecture.

The Symbolic Serial Processing System

An overwhelming majority of philosophers subsrcibe to the classical computational architecture, which is a sequential symbol-manipulating device. This device has got two aspects — (a) representation, and (b) manipulation or transition or algorithm.

(a) In the representation part there are structured symbols, i.e. symbols that designate something. Designation is one of the core ideas of computing. Symbols may designate in several ways — they can provide access to other symbols, they can cause an interpreter to perform the action designated by that symbol, or they may designate extrinsic things. They may designate, for example, abstract objects like numbers, or they may designate objects of reasoning, or they may even designate goals. So the symbolic

7 See Newell and Simon, 1963, "Computers in Psychology".

8 Rich, 1983, *Artificial Intelligence.*

expressions have a semantics.

(b) The transition part consists of some rules that transform a sequence of symbols to another in a systematic way. The way such structured symbols are transformed is very important. The transformations of the symbols are so designed that the semantics of the symbols is coherently maintained.

Newell et al. have made the following list of the functions, known so far, of this architecture:[9]

1. Memory
   (a) Contains structures that contain symbol tokens.
   (b) Independently modifiable at some grain size.
   (c) Sufficient memory.
2. Symbols
   (a) Patterens that provide access to distal symbol structures.
   (b) A symbol token in the occurance of a pattern in a structure.
   (c) Sufficient symbols.
3. Operations
   (a) Processes that take symbol structures as input and produce symbol structures as output.
   (b) Complete compossibility.
4. Interpretation
   (a) Processes that take symbol structures as input and produce behaviour by executing operations.
   (b) Complete interpretability.
5. Interaction with the external world
   (a) Perceptual and motor interfaces.
   (b) Buffering and interruptions.

[9] Newell, Rosenbloom and Laird, 1996, "Symbolic Architectures for Congnition".

(c) Real-time demands for action.

(d) Continuous acquisition of knowledge.

Cognitive scientists have constructed many symbolic architectures of cognition. Act[10] is the first theory of such an architecture. A more recent symbolic architecture is Soar.[11] *Fig.* 7.1 gives the basic structure of Soar and provides an overview of it. There is single long-term memory — a production system that is used for both declarative and procedural knowledge. There is a working memory that contains a goal hierarchy, information associated with the goal hierarchy, preferences about what should be done, perceptual information, and motor commands. Interaction with the outside world occurs via interfaces between working memory and one or more perceptual and motor systems. Encoded symbolic structures received in the working memory as input from the perceptual system activate some distal symbol

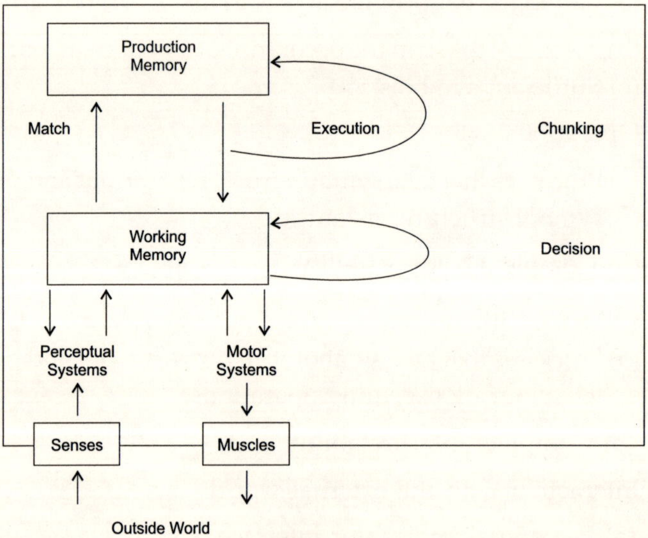

fig. 7.1

[10] See Anderson, 1983, *The Architecture of Cognition*.

[11] Laird and Rosenbloon, 1987, "Soar: An Architecture for General Intelligence".

structures in the long-term memory through pattern matching. The production system then applies relevant operations on the activated symbol structures and produces new symbol structures. Thereafter the working memory makes decisions on the basis of the productions retrieved from the production system. Finally, the working memory uses its relevant motor commands and yields decoded output in the external world.

In the above symbolic architecture the entire computation, starting from the input up to the output, takes place serially. Subsequently questions have been raised about the biological plausibility of this architecture. Feldman points out[12] that in human organism neurons operate in the scale of milliseconds, whereas in a serial computer computer-components operate in the time scale of nanoseconds — a factor of 10^6 faster. This means that human cognitive processes that take on the order of a second or less can involve only one hunderd or so time steps. It is experimentally proved that most of the human cognitive processes — perception, memory retrieval, speech processing, sentence comprehension and the like — take about a second or so. Hence 100-steps constraint should be imposed on the processing in order to make it biologically plausible. The classical computational architecture encounters some other difficulties as well. So cognitive scientists are in search of alternative computational architecture. Rumelhart[13] has proposed on alternative computational architecture, which, he claims, can avoid the problems encountered by the classical serial computing device. This new architecture is known as "the parallel distributed processing device". The theory suggesting the basic structure of such an architecture is called "connectionism". The basic strategy of the connectionist approach is to take as its fundamental processing unit something close to an abstract neuron. It is imagined that computation is carried out through simple interactions among such processing units. So this alternative processing is also called "neural processing".

---

12 Feldman, 1985, "Connectionist Models and their Applications".

13 Rumelhart, 1997, "The Architecture of Mind: A Connectionist Approach".

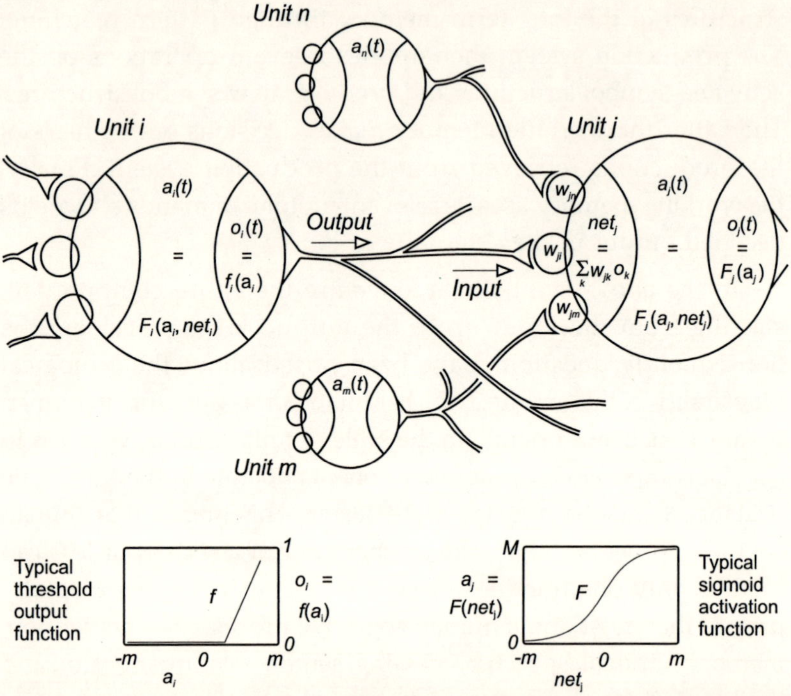

fig. 7.2

Connectionist systems are large networks of extremely simple processors, massively interconnected and running in parallel. Each processor has a numerical activation value that it communicates to other processors along connections of varying strengths. The activation value for each processor constantly changes in response to the activity of the processors to which it is connected. The values of some of the processors form the input to the system, and the values of processors form the output. The connections between the processors determine how input is transformed to the output. In connectionist systems knowledge is encoded not in symbolic structures, but rather in the pattern of numerical strengths of the connections between processors. *Fig.* 7.2 gives an overview of a parallel distributed processing system.[14]

Rumelhart distinguishes seven major components of any

[14] Rmelhart, 1997, op. cit.

connectionist system:

i. set of *processing units;*

ii. a state of *activation* denied over the processing units;

iii. an *output function* for each unit that maps its state of activation into an output;

iv. a *pattern of connectivity* among untis;

v. an *activation rule* for combining the inputs impinging on a unit with its current state to produce a new level of activation for the unit;

vi. a *learning rule* whereby patterns of connectivity are modified by experience; and

vii. an *environment* within which the system must operate.

Fig. 7.2 illustrates the basic aspects of any connectionist system. The set of processing units are indicated by circles in the diagram. Specifying the set of processing units and what they represent is typically the first stage of specifying a connectionist model. In some systems these units may represent particular conceptual objects such as features, letters, words or concepts; in others they are simply abstract elements over which meaningful patterns can be defined. At each point in time each unit U_i has an activation value, denoted in the diagram as $a_i(t)$. The output value passes through a set of unidirectional connections, indicated by lines or arrows in the diagram, to other units in the system. There is associated with each connection a real number, usually called the weight or strength of the connection, designated as *wij* (to unit *i* from unit *j*) which determines how strongly the former is affected by the latter. All of the inputs then get combined, and the combined inputs to a unit (usually designated as the *net input* to that unit) along with its current activation value, determine its new activation value via a function *F*.

8

Wittgenstein on Necessity and Objectivity in Mathematics and Logic

WITTGENSTEIN'S philosophy of mathematics and logic haunts every researcher in this area although a very few succeed eventually, the history shows, to enter into this majestic castle. The present paper is an attempt to have a clear view of this castle, though it may turn out to be an usual failure, through the deep fog surrounding it.

Much of the dispute among commentators vis-à-vis the nature of mathematics and logic concerns whether Wittgenstein was a realist or an anti-realist. Although Wittgenstein is normally read as an anti-realist concerning mathematics and logic there are oppositions to this reading, e.g. Cora Diamond is devoted to argue against anti-realist readings of Wittgenstein's philosophy of mathematics.[1] Before entering into this prolonged debate let me put it very clearly the sense in which the issue of realism is understood throughout this chapter.

The word "realism" is no more used as a blanket term. The talk of realism *simpliciter* is now replaced by the talk of realism concerning a specific subject matter. So the concept of realism is relativized to a certain class of entities. Michael Dummett has given a new formulation of realism by relativizing it to a class of statements instead of a class of entities.[2] This turn from entity to language marks the present-day discussion on realism. The peculiarity of a realism concerning a class of statements consists, says Dummett, in maintaining the objectivity of the statements of

---

1 Diamond, 1991, *Realism and the Realistic Spirit*.

2 Dummett, 1981, "Realism".

this class. The word "realism" is used in this paper in this Dummettian sense. So, when it is asked "Is Wittgenstein a realist or an anti-realist concerning mathematics and logic?", what is intended is whether Wittgenstein maintains the objectivity of mathematical and logical statements or not.

Using a coinage of John McDowell, Putnam characterizes the debate on objectivity in his *Dewey Lectures*[3] published in 1994 as the recoil phenomenon: an oscillation between two extreme positions, with each camp reacting to the untenable part of the other, resulting, finally, in two untenable positions. On one side of the divide are those who deny objectivity in all fields. They hold that there are only incommensurable narratives. On the other side of the divide are those who attempt to secure objectivity, but do so at the cost of clothing it in metaphysical mystery.

> The first side points out the illusions in the second's metaphysics and then recoils to anarchy. The second shows the inherent contradictions in the anarchist position, and then recoils to build more epicycles in its metaphysical castle.[4]

Wittgenstein's philosophy of mathematics and logic should be understood in the background of this recoil phenomenon of objectivity.

Philosophers belong to the objectivity camp picture mathematics as transcendent: a mathematical proposition has truth and meaning regardless of human rules and use. There is an underlying mathematical reality which is independent of our mathematical practice and language and which adjudicates the correctness of that practice and language. One of the most influential personalities in this camp is the famous mathematician G.H. Hardy ("Wittgenstein on Necessity and Objectivity in Mathematics" in *A Mathematician's Apology*).[5] He says:

---

3 See Putnam 1997; and 1994 "Science, Non-sense, and the Senses", pp. 445-517.

4 Gerrard, 1996, "A Philosophy of Mathematics between Two Camps", p. 171.

5 Hardy, 1967, *A Mathematician's Apology*.

> I believe that mathematical reality lies outside us, that our function is to discover or observe it, and that the theorems that we prove, and which we describe grandiloquently as our 'creations', are simply our notes of our observations.

Another renowned personality belonging to this camp is Gottlob Frege, a Platonist, who holds that logical and mathematical truths like "$\neg(P\&\neg P)$" and "2 + 2 = 4" are necessary and objective and that this objectivity can only be secured by assuming that their subject matters are not private ideas in the minds of individuals, but abstract entities inhabiting, a third realm beyond space and time.

Bertrand Russell too says that logical propositions are completely general truths about the most pervasive traits of reality.

All of the positions mentioned so far assume that mathematics and logic are sciences which make statements about entities of some kind, just as empirical sciences make statements about physical objects.

At the beginning of Wittgenstein's career the anarchist camp would have been exemplified by a view called psychologism. Mathematicians and logicians like George Boole belonging to this camp hold that the laws of logic describe how human beings (by and large) think, their basic mental operations, and these laws are determined by the nature of the human mind.

The exemplars of the objectivity camp combated psychologism, ". . . 317 is a prime" Hardy asserted, "not because we think so, or because our minds are shaped in one way rather than another, but because it is so, because mathematical reality is built that way".[6] Frege and Russell believed that identifying the laws of logic with the laws of psychology would necessarily lead to a complete loss of objectivity. Frege's *Grundgesetze*[7] contains a typical argument for the route from psychologism to anarchy:

---

[6] Hardy, 1967, op. cit., p. 130.

[7] Frege, 1964, *The Basic Laws of Arithmetic*, p. xix.

> If we could not grasp anything but what was within our own selves, then a conflict of opinions [based on] a mutual understanding would be impossible, because a common ground would be lacking, and no idea in the psychological sense can afford us such a ground. There would be no logic to be appointed arbiter in the conflict of opinions.

Wittgenstein has criticized vehemently the assumption of the objectivity camp that mathematical and logical propositions describe a sophisticated reality of which we can have special experience. The fundamental thought of the *Tractatus Logico Philosophicus* (*TLP*) is that this assumption is false.[8] Wittgenstein attacks Frege's and Russell's idea that the logical particles occurring in a logical statement are names of entities (functions inhabiting a Platonic realm in the former case and "logical objects" with which we are acquainted through logical experience in the latter). The role of logical particles, he says, is not to name objects of any kind. In *TLP* he says:

> My fundamental idea is that the "logical constants" are not representatives; . . . — 4.0312

He also says:

> At this point it becomes manifest that there are no "logical objects" or "logical constants" (in Frege's and Russell's sense). — *TLP* 5.4

Since there is no logical object, logical statements cannot be about entities. The role of logical statements is not to describe reality lying out there. "The propositions of mathematics", says Wittgenstein, "are equations, and therefore pseudo-propositions" (*TLP* 6.2). Mathematical propositions being pseudo-propositions are not descriptions of anything at all. Wittgenstein never wavered from rejecting the metaphysical picture of the objectivity camp.

---

[8] See Wittgenstein, 1961b, *Tractatus Logico-Philosophicus*, 5.552-5.5571. Also see Chakraborti, Somnath, 1998, "Tractatus-e-Maulobakya Prasanga". Sri Chakraborti has reformulated Wittgenstein's argument against this assumption.

Wittgenstein's rejection of the underlying assumption of the objectivity camp in the historical background sketched above may naturally suggest that he was a philosopher of the anarchist camp. But this suggestion is palpably wrong. Wittgenstein never rejected his predecessors' anti-psychologism. Frege linked his context principle with his fight against psychologism. In the *Foundations of Arithmetic*[9] Frege has explained how psychologism arises out of the violation of the context principle throughout his philosophical career. He says, "an expression has meaning only in a proposition" (*TLP* 3.314). So he emphasized his opposition to psychologism as did Hardy, Frege and Russell. He believed that Frege had satisfactorily smashed the anarchist camp in its psychologistic form.

Thus, we see that since Wittgenstein opposes psychologism, he would say that mathematical and logical statements do not possess subjectivity: the Law of Non-contradiction $\neg,(P\&\neg, p)$, for example, is not a statement about the way people actually think. He also opposes, as we have seen, the Hardyan objectivity of mathematical and logical statements. So the question naturally arises: Did Wittgenstein deny the necessity and objectivity of mathematical and logical statements altogether? The answer is uprightly no. Wittgenstein had no doubt about the necessity and objectivity of mathematical and logical statements. His problem was how to account for it. The Hardy–Frege–Russell way of explaining the necessity and objectivity of mathematical and logical statements was not acceptable to Wittgenstein.

So he raises the question in *Remarks on the Foundations of Mathematics*[10] (*RFM*):

> But then what does the peculiar inexorability of mathematics consist in?

Wittgenstein gives an account of the necessity and objectivity of mathematical and logical statements by relating them to linguistic rules. According to him, these statements do not describe a special

---

[9] Frege, 1953, *The Foundations of Arithmetic*, sect. 60, p. 71.

[10] Wittgenstein, 1956, *Remarks on the Foundations of Mathematics*, sect. 4.

kind of reality, but reflect linguistic rules. These statements are not descriptive, they are normative. The necessity and objectivity of these statements are, says Wittgenstein, due to their normativity.

The development of Wittgenstein's philosophy of mathematics and logic is found through certain stages. Steve Gerrard in his 1996 article,[11] has distinguished, three stages of the development: early, middle and later. The early stage is found in *Notebooks 1914-1916*[12] and *TLP*. The middle period view dominated Wittgenstein's thought from 1929 through the early 1930s. Wittgenstein's view at this stage is called by Gerrard "the calculus conception" and it is mostly found in *Philosophical Grammar* (*PG*).[13] The later stage starts from the middle of 1930s. *Philosophical Investigations* (*PI*),[14] *LFM*,[15] *RFM*[16] contain Wittgenstein's thought of the later stage.

One common thread of Wittgenstein's account of necessity and objectivity of mathematical and logical statements is that the special status of these statements is not due to the peculiar character of what they represent, but due to the fact that they are linked to rules which provide the pre-empirical framework of representation. They reflect the necessary preconditions of this representation. Wittgenstein argues that mathematical and logical propositions look like experiential propositions which are descriptive in nature, but actually the relations of mathematical and logical statements to reality are entirely different from that of experiential propositions. The similarities of grammatical appearance of these two kinds of proposition seriously misled philosophers like Hardy, Frege and Russell of the objectivity camp as well as the exemplars of the anarchist camp to treat mathematical and logical statements as descriptive.

---

11 Gerrard, 1996, op. cit.

12 Wittgenstein, 1961a, *Notebooks 1914-16*.

13 Wittgenstein, 1974, *Philosophical Grammar*.

14 Wittgenstein, 1973, *Philosophical Investigations*.

15 Diamond (ed.), 1993, *Wittgenstein's Lectures on the Foundations of Mathematics*.

16 Wittgenstein, 1956, op. cit.

It is unfortunate that Lovibond associates homogeneity of language with Wittgenstein's philosophy. In *Realism and Imagination in Ethics*[17] she says:

> What Wittgenstein offers us . . . is a homogeneous or "seamless" conception of language. It is a conception free from invidious comparisons between different regions of discourse . . . just as the early Wittgenstein considers all propositions to be of equal value . . . , so the later Wittgenstein . . . regards all *language games* as being of "equal value". . . .

Wittgenstein did say "all propositions are of equal value" in *TLP* 6.4. But this should be read in conjunction with his other remarks in *TLP* like "the propositions of mathematics are . . . pseudo-propositions" (*TLP* 6.2). The propositions of logic are tautologies. Therefore, "the propositions of logic say nothing" (*TLP* 6.1, 6.11).

All that Wittgenstein intends to say is that all genuine propositions are of equal value and their equality consists in the depiction of reality. Mathematical and logical propositions are not genuine propositions, they do not depict or describe reality at all. Wittgenstein holds that the special status of these necessary propositions is due to the fact that they reflect the necessary preconditions for depicting reality.

The position of Wittgenstein has a striking similarity with that of Kant who holds that mathematical judgements are possible in so far as they express necessary preconditions for experiencing objects. But there are differences between these two positions. In contrast to Kant, Wittgenstein would say that these preconditions no longer reside in a mental machinery. Again, unlike Kant, Wittgenstein is of the opinion that mathematical propositions are analytic.

One may try to find an analogy of Wittgenstein's position with logical positivism. The goal of logical positivists was to account for logical and mathematical necessity without reducing it to empirical generality, lapsing into Platonism or admitting synthetic

[17] Lovibond, 1983, *Realism and Imagination in Ethics*.

a priori truth. According to the logical positivists, necessary propositions are analytic, i.e. true solely in virtue of the meanings of their constituent words.

Wittgenstein's position cannot be identified with that of logical positivists. In fact, these two positions are, in one respect, diametrically opposite. The contrast between Wittgenstein's position and that of logical positivists has been explained by Amitabha Dasgupta in terms of compositionality and growth.[18] Dasgupta argues that in the positivist theory meaning is compositional whereas in Wittgenstein's theory it is not so. Again, the positivist conception of mathematics fails to explain the growth of mathematics, whereas Wittgenstein's conception succeeds to explain it. But I think that this way of showing the contrast between Wittgenstein's position and that of logical positivists concerning logico-mathematical necessity cannot show the real contrast between the two positions. The real contrast can be shown in the following way. Unlike logical positivists, Wittgenstein would not say that the meanings of the constituents determine the necessity of logico-mathematical statements. Rather these statements give meaning to the constituents. The key to understanding the status of necessary propositions is the concept of a grammatical rule. Grammatical rules are standards for the correct use of a word which determine its meaning.[19] The linguistic appearance of logico-mathematical statements is that of statements of fact, but their actual role is that of grammatical rules. It is the normative character of these statements, says Wittgenstein, which determine their necessity. By making the rules do all the work, Wittgenstein was trying to avoid both psychologism and Hardy's underlying mathematical reality. This also helps to exhibit the differences between his position and those of Kant and logical positivists.

---

[18] Dasgupta, 1992, "Wittgenstein on Mathematical Necessity".

(a) Wittgenstein, 1993, *Philosophical Occasions*, p. 51.

(b) Wittgenstein, 1969, *On Certainty*, pp. 61-62.

(c) Wittgenstein, 1974, op. cit., p. 337.

[19] Dummett, 1978c, "Wittgenstein's Philosophy of Mathematics".

Wittgenstein's grammatical perspective concerning logico-mathematical necessity has been misinterpreted by Dummett as a full-blooded conventionalism, a variety of anarchism.[20] According to Dummett, Wittgenstein believes that the logico-mathematical necessity of any statement is always the direct expression of a linguistic convention. It is not that our calculations and proofs follow from an antecedent set of agreed upon conventions, but that at every step a new decision is required. So the misinterpretation goes like this. By denying the picture of an underlying mathematical reality, through his anthropological method, by stressing the contingent factors that yield our logico-mathematical language and by claiming that at each step the calculations or proofs could have been otherwise Wittgenstein reduced logico-mathematical necessity to the level of the conventional. It is as if Frege saved us from psychologism only to have Wittgenstein deliver us to sociologism.

Wittgenstein foresaw this possible misinterpretation. "What you say", writes Wittgenstein in *RFM*, assuming the voice of someone who has misinterpreted what has gone before,

> seems to amount to this, that logic belongs to the natural history of man. And that is not combinable with the hardness of the logical "must".[21]

That Wittgenstein did not assimilate, unlike Locke, the logico-mathematical propositions to the proposition of natural history escaped the notice of Dummett. In *RFM* Wittgenstein says:

> But the logical "must" is a component part of the propositions of logic, and these are not propositions of human natural history. If what a proposition of logic said was: Human beings agree with one another in such and such ways (and that would be the form of the natural historical proposition), then its contradictory would say that there is here a lack of agreement. Not, that there is an agreement of another kind.[22]

---

[20] Wittgenstein, 1956, op. cit., VI-49A.

[21] Ibid., VI-49.

[22] (a) Quinton, 1973, *The Nature of Things*, pp. 216-17.

→

It should be noted here that in *TLP* and other earlier writings Wittgenstein treated mathematical and logical statements as pseudo-propositions in the sense that they do not describe reality, rather they reflect the necessary preconditions for depicting reality. At this earlier stage he did not clearly explain what determines the necessity and objectivity of mathematical and logical statements. It is in the middle period that he clearly stated that the necessity and objectivity under consideration are determined by the normativity of the statements concerned.

But what exactly does Wittgenstein intend to say when he says that mathematical and logical statements give meaning to the components of these statements? Let us explain it with an example. "$P \rightarrow \neg\neg p$" is regarded as a logical statement which is necessary indeed. One may hold, like a logical positivist, that the necessity of the statement depends upon the meaning given to by the following truth table:

p	$\neg P$
T	F
F	$T1$

If this is the meaning of "$\neg$" then when p is true "$\neg p$" will be false and in that case "$\neg\neg p$" will be true. So, if "p" is true then "$\neg\neg p$" must be true [$P \rightarrow \neg\neg p$]. Wittgenstein does not admit this way of explaining the necessity of logical statement. He wants to say that "$p \rightarrow \neg\neg p$" gives meaning to the logical constant "$\neg$"; it is a rule giving meaning to "$\neg$". It prescribes how to use "$\neg$". In all experimental situations we simply follow this rule. The logical statements are viewed by Wittgenstein as rules which license transformations of experiential statements. Similarly, mathematical statements prescribe the use of mathematical operations which we simply follow in experiential situations. As logical and mathematical statements antecede experience in an innocuous

← (b) Dummett, 1973, *Frege: Philosophy of Language*, pp. 596-601.

(c) Wright, 1980, *Wittgenstein on the Foundations of Mathematics*, pp. 329-30.

sense, they can neither be confirmed nor be confuted by experience. This peculiar kind of antecedence, which is different from Kant's, as pointed out earlier, renders intelligible the apparently mysterious "hardness" of necessary propositions. So, according to Wittgenstein, mathematics and logic as such are always measure, not things measured. We follow them to judge experience, not experience to judge them.

Wittgenstein's rejection of the logical positivistic account of logico-mathematical statements as analytic in the sense that they are necessarily true by virtue of the meaning of their components brings him very close to Quine. Quine questions the very notion of analyticity as advocated by the logical positivists. He shows that this notion belongs to a cluster of intentional concepts including "synonymy", "self-contradiction", "necessity", "definition" and "semantic rule". These concepts cannot be defined without using other members of this family. Quine thinks that this amounts to a vicious circularity.

Despite this similarity Wittgenstein's position must be contrasted with that of Quine. For Quine, logic and mathematics are meaningful by virtue of their being connected with experience and truth or the falsity of logical and mathematical statements is determined by the success or failure of predictions, made on the basis of them, from scientific theories. According to Quine, there is no qualitative difference between logico-mathematical statements and empirical statements. The only difference between them admitted by Quine is that in the holistic web of beliefs the logico-mathematical beliefs occupy the central position and the empirical ones occupy its periphery. This only means that we are more reluctant to abandon the former beliefs. Wittgenstein by contrast, advocates necessity of logico-mathematical statements which empirical propositions are lacking. And, to repeat, the necessity of them is determined by their normativity. So Wittgenstein is opposed to Quine's reductionism.

Quinton, Dummett and Crispin Wright argue that Quine's assimilation of logico-mathematical statements to the empirical ones sits uneasily with his own holistic picture of a web of beliefs.[23] Recently Hans-Johann Glock observes in "Necessity and Normativity"[24] that a collection of beliefs can only be woven into a web if certain propositions are not merely abandoned with greater reluctance, but can play a different role, viz. that of establishing logical connections between different beliefs.

Thus, we see that Wittgenstein gives a kind of autonomy to logic and mathematics. Experiential statements are descriptive and are answerable to or justified by logico-mathematical statements which look like descriptive ones but actually they are rules. These rules do not need further justification. They are self-justifying because they are meaning-giving. This was Wittgenstein's position in the middle period of his philosophical career. Such a position is known as formalism.

Arthur Prior has raised a serious objection, in his article "The Run About Inference Ticket",[25] to the unrestricted licence for whatever logical laws one chooses. He argues that this may render the entire language inconsistent. His example is a binary connective "*" having its introduction rules in common with "or" and its elimination rules in common with "and" From "*P*" we may derive "*P***Q*" by the help of the introduction rule for "*"; then we can derive *Q* from "*P***Q*" by the help of the elimination rule for "*". Similarly, we can derive "$\neg Q$" from "*p*". So we can derive "$Q\& \neg Q$" from "*P*" by the help of the introduction rule for "&". Thus, the rules for "*" yield a contradiction. Hence, if logic is given absolute autonomy then our language will be full of contradictions.

Belnap, Dummett and others who share the view with Wittgenstein that logical rules are self-justifying, have imposed certain most general restrictions on logical rules. Belnap has mentioned in his article "Tonk, Plonk and Plink"[26] two restrictions,

---

[23] Hans-Johann, 1996, "Necessity and Normativity".

[24] Prior, 1960, "The Run About Inference Ticket".

[25] Belnap, 1962, "Tonk, Plonk and Plink".

[26] Dummett, 1991, *The Logical Basis* of *Metaphysics*.

viz. conservative extension and uniqueness. Dummett has imposed a further condition, viz. stability.[27] They have explained how by the imposition of these restrictions the above kind of inconsistency can be avoided.

Wittgenstein, being a genius, anticipated this kind of undesirable consequence of his formalism advocated in the middle period of his philosophical career. But he did not follow the line of thought as found in Belnap and Dummett for avoiding the consequence. In the later period he revised his position. In this period he feels that the logical and mathematical rules require some kind of justification. In *LFM* he says:

> If we allow contradictions in such a way that we accept that anything follows, then we would no longer get a calculus, or we'd get a useless thing resembling a calculus.[28]

For the justification of logico-mathematical rules Wittgenstein relates logico-mathematical language, in his later period, to *language-games* and ultimately to our form of life. In *RFM* he says:

> The rules of logical inference are rules of the language-game.[29]

In *PI* Wittgenstein has given a detailed account of language-game which is presupposed here. It should be kept in mind that even in the later period Wittgenstein has retained the normative character of logic and mathematics. Even in *RFM* we find him to say:

> We can conceive the rules of inference — I want to say — as giving the signs their meaning, because they are rules for the use of these signs. So that the rules of inference are involved in the determination of the meaning of the signs. In this sense rules of inference cannot be right or wrong.[30]

In *RFM* he also remarks:

---

[27] Wittgenstein, 1939, *Lectures on the Foundations of Mathematics*, p. 243.

[28] Wittgenstein, 1978, *Remarks on the Foundations of Mathematics*, V28.

[29] Ibid., V23.

[30] Ibid., V40.

> What I am saying comes to this, that mathematics is normative.[31]

So the necessity and objectivity are retained even in Wittgenstein's later period. And here also he says that the necessity and objectivity of logic and mathematics are due to their normativity. But what is new in this period is that the logical and mathematical rules are tied down to the language-game. He holds that logic and mathematics form networks of norms and they are parts of a family of language-games. The logico-mathematical rules which we follow in this family of language games cannot be altered once these rules are laid down and practised.[32] No new rule can be introduced which conflict with this family. Herein lie the necessity and objectivity of mathematics and logic. Given the background of a family of language-game, mathematical and logical statements are not revisable. By contrast, experimental statements are revisable even within this family of language-game.

This feature of non-revisability distinguishes Wittgenstein's position concerning logic and mathematics from that of intuitionism. It should also be noticed that although Wittgenstein related the legitimacy of logico-mathematical rules to our practice, his position should not be identified with pragmatism; because in pragmatism logico-mathematical propositions are revisable, but it is not admitted by Wittgenstein. Thus, Wittgenstein's position concerning logic and mathematics should be distinguished from descriptivism as advocated by Hardy–Frege–Russell camp as well as from psychologism. It should also be distinguished from the position of Kant and that of logical positivists. It is also illegitimate to identify his position with Quinean reductionism or Dummettian verificationism. Neither, it is legitimate to identify his position with intuitionism or pragmatism.

A further question arises here. The question is:

> Are logico-mathematical statements revisable outside a family

---

31 Wittgenstein, 1978, op. cit., V31.

32 Ibid., V23.

> of language-game?" One interpretation of Wittgenstein's philosophy is that there can be alternative different families of language-game in which logic and mathematics form different networks of norms. So although logico-mathematical statements are necessary within a family of language-games, they are contingent from the externalist point of view. Perhaps this kind of interpretation led W.W. Tait to observe that "necessity rides on the back of contingency.

Another interpretation is that the necessity of logico-mathematical statements is ultimately tied down to the constitution of human mind and under the present constitution of it no change of logico-mathematical rules is possible. Philosophers who give this interpretation take to distinguish a fourth and last period of Wittgenstein's philosophy which was dominated by his philosophy of psychology. Here I do not like to enter into this debate.

So, what I see throughout the three stages of the development of Wittgenstein's philosophy of logic and mathematics is that according to him, logico-mathematical statements are necessary and objective. Since Wittgenstein advocates necessity and objectivity of logic and mathematics he should be regarded as a realist so far as logic and mathematics are concerned. But the distinctive feature of his realism consists in the belief that the necessity and objectivity of logicomathematical statements are due to their normativity, he says in *RFM*:

> Not empiricism and yet realism in philosophy, that is the hardest thing.[33]

[33] Wittgenstein, 1978, op. cit., V23.

9

Truth, Meaning and Understanding
The Dummett–Davidson Controversy

Meaning and Communication

A COMMON assumption among philosophers of language is that one of the principal functions of language is communication, although they differ on the issue of primacy of this function.[1] A principal task of a philosopher is to give a satisfactory account of how we communicate. Some philosophers attempt to illuminate how we communicate by appeal to a clearly defined shared structure which language users acquire. Davidson is one of those who give up the idea of clearly defined shared structure for giving an account of communication.[2] Sibajiban Bhattacharyya argues that it is impossible to account for the common understanding in communication without a clearly defined shared structure of language. Bhattacharya says:

> If the speaker has the freedom to use any word to mean what he chooses then the speaker has the freedom to invent whatever words he chooses. This freedom will turn a language into a private language; so to make language a tool of intersubjective, words have to be used in their conventional, i.e. semantic sense.[3]

This observation of Bhattacharyya is based on his distinction between the speaker's intended meaning of a sentence in communication and the semantic meaning of it. Bhattacharyya rightly observes that the former meaning is partly determined by

---

[1] Dummett, 1989, "Language and Communication".

[2] Davidson, 1986c, "A Nice Derangement of Epitaphs".

[3] Bhattacharyya, 1997, "Introduction to the Navya-Nyāya Theory of Language".

the latter meaning. But he is wrong to suppose that Davidson is concerned with the speaker's intended meaning as opposed to the semantic meaning or literal meaning of a sentence used for communication.[4] Davidson is rather engaged in exploring our apparatus in communicating the literal meaning of a sentence of a language. In order to account for the speaker's intended meaning we have to add a pragmatic apparatus to it. Davidson has given an account of communication of the literal meaning of sentences of a language without invoking a shared structure.

Meaning and Understanding

In an ideal instance of communication of the literal meaning of a sentence a speaker uses a sentence in a particular context and the hearer understands it. So to give an account of communication of the literal meaning of the sentences of a language is to explain our understanding of it. Thus for Davidson a theory of communication of the literal meaning of the sentences of a language, in short, the theory of meaning for a language, is a theory of understanding of it. Davidson proposes that the study of meaning is best approached via theories of meaning. In the early 1960s, the philosophy of language was radically altered when Davidson redefined both what form a meaning theory for a natural language can take and what condition of adequacy, both empirical and formal, such theories should meet. Along with Quine, he discouraged philosophers from analysing such individual concepts as meaning. Instead, he framed questions about meaning theory in the context of understanding language. In this context he draws a distinction between theory of meaning and meaning theory. He calls the kind of theory a philosopher of language advocates as "theory of meaning", and the theory a field linguist is concerned with as "meaning theory". A meaning theory is concerned with a specific language, whereas a philosopher aims at developing a theory of meaning that specifies what meaning theories for specific languages lay bare. So a philosopher's theory of meaning, which,

4 Bhattacharyya, 1997, op. cit.

according to Davidson, is a theory of understanding, is a second order theory.

J.L. Shaw has criticized the attempt to identify a theory of meaning with a theory of understanding. He points out that the Nyāya has drawn a distinction between "the meaning of a sentence or a complex expression" and "the understanding of the meaning of a sentence or complex expression". The latter expression means the understanding of the relation that is due to the syntactic competency between the expression (*anvaya-bodha*). It refers to the cognition generated by a sentence or complex expression. The conditions for understanding the meaning of a sentence would include semantic competency (*yogyatā*) between the referents of the expressions which occur in a sentence and the spatio-temporal continuity or proximity (*sannidhi*) between these expressions in addition to the syntactic competency (*anvaya-bodha*) between the expressions. For this reason, according to the Nyāya, the sentences like "He irrigates the field with fire", "*a* is *a*" and "An *a* which is *F* is not *F*" do not generate any cognition in the hearer or the speaker, although they are meaningful sentences, and each of them would receive a truth value, i.e. truth or falsity.[5] Dummett, and Davidson as well, would make a distinction in this context between a truth theory and a meaning theory for a language. A truth theory specifics truth conditions for the sentences of a language, whereas a meaning theory gives an account of the understanding of the language. The truth theory and the meaning theory for a language are closely related although they are different. Demmett observes that the former constitutes the base of the latter. A proposed truth theory for a language can be justified if a satisfactory meaning theory for the language can be constructed on the basis of it.

Davidson's Pro-theory Approach

In philosophy of language the various approaches to meaning can broadly be classified into (a) pro-theory approach, and (b) anti-theory approach. Later Wittgenstein's approach to meaning, for

[5] Shaw, 1985, "Proper Names: Contemporary Philosophy and the Nyāya".

example, is anti-theory approach whereas Noam Chomsky's approach to meaning is pro-theory approach. Later Wittgenstein does not admit that a competent speaker of a language possesses a meaning theory. By contrast Chomsky admits a specific Language Acquisition Device (LAD) in a human being by the use of which a speaker of a language develops a meaning theory for the language when she learns it. Davidson's approach to meaning belongs to the latter kind. Behaviourists characterize understanding of language in terms of behaviour-linguistic and non-linguistic. Davidson holds that characterizing understanding of language in terms of linguistic and non-linguistic behaviours is inadequate. Davidson adheres to John Searle's famous Chinese room argument. A speaker of a language can have a capacity to exhibit appropriate linguistic and non-linguistic behaviour without having any understanding of the language under consideration.[6] The behaviouristic theory cannot account for the creativity of a language user. Within a short period of time a speaker of a language can generate many sentences and use them appropriately although she has never come across the use of those sentences.[7] According to Davidson, understanding of a language consists in the possession of a meaning theory for that language. Davidson's position regarding understanding of a language is better understood if the context of understanding it is taken to be foreign to the learner. The learner encounters a situation in which people around her communicate in a language foreign to her, and she is to decipher from their use of their language the meaning of it. Davidson says that after a long journey through a plethora of probabilities the learner arrives at a theory, which he calls his meaning theory for the language, the possession of which constitutes his understanding of the language. Is this meaning theory identical with the meaning theory of the native speaker on the basis of whose use of the language the learner has arrived at the theory? At an early stage of the development of his thoughts

---

6 Searle, 1980, "Minds, Brains and Programs".

7 Chomsky, 1964, "A Review of B.F. Skinner's Verbal Behaviour".

about understanding of language Davidson is found to adhere to the identity thesis, but at the later stage he seems to hold that we do not have legitimate ground to say that the meaning theory developed by the learner is identical with that of the native speaker. The more legitimate claim would be, according to Davidson, that learner's meaning theory is like that of the native speaker.

Davidson's Truth-theoretic Account of Understanding of Language

The kind of theory by the possession of which constitutes a speaker's understanding of a language is, according to Davidson, a Tarski-type truth theory for that language. Such a theory specifies truth conditions of the sentences of the language. Although the meaning theory takes the form of truth theory in Tarski's style, it differs in style, it differs from the truth theory in its intention. The truth theory for a language intends to specify the condition for truth of every sentence of the language, whereas the meaning theory intends to specify meaning for the sentences of it. In a Tarski-type theory the notion of synonymy or translation is presupposed. Tarski uses the notion of translation in formulating the condition of material adequacy for any truth theory. A meaning theory will be accused of involving a vicious circle if it uses the concept of translation, and so it will fail to have the explanatory power it is expected of.

Formal and Empirical Constraints on a Davidsonian Meaning Theory

If a meaning theory for a language is to be developed in the style of a Tarski-type truth theory then such a theory has to satisfy a formal constraint. A Tarski-type theory for a language is a finitely axiomatized theory. It specifies truth condition for every sentence of the language on the basis of recursive definition of satisfaction for the sentential functions of the language. This recursive definition of satisfaction rests on the Fregean syntactic structure of the language for which the truth theory is to be given. Thus in order to develop a meaning theory for a language in the style of a Tarski-type truth theory, the language must have the same Fregean syntactic structure as any formal language for the quantification theory has. Davidson says, ". . . the result of applying the formal constraints is, then, to fit the object language as a whole to the Procrustean bed of quantification theory".[8] A meaning theory developed for a language in the style of a Tarski-type must also satisfy an empirical constraint. Since such a meaning theory is an empirical theory it must have an empirical content, i.e. the truth conditions that the meaning theory attaches to the sentences must have an experiential basis.

Radical Interpretation as the Basis of Davidsonian Meaning Theory

According to Davidson, the empirical content of a meaning theory for a language is provided by radical interpretation. Radical interpretation is an interpretation because it is a process that relates sentences of a language to the world: it is radical because the only clue that is available for this kind of interpretation is that the competent speaker (of the language under consideration) holds a given sentence true in a certain circumstance. The aim of a meaning theory for a language is to assign those truth conditions to the sentences of the language that the competent speaker assigns to them. The entire meaning theory is built on the basis of assent and dissent of the competent speaker of the language for which the meaning theory is developed. Consider the simple sentence "There's a table". Our basic clue for assigning truth condition to this sentence is that the speaker is caused to assent (not just on this occasion, but generally) to this sentence by the presence of table, while the absence of table causes him, generally) to dissent from the same sentence.

Belief–Meaning Interlocking

We have seen that the aim of the Davidsonain meaning theory or

[8] Davidson, 1984, *Inquiries into Truth and Interpretation.*

a language is to specify truth condition for the sentences of the languages that the competent speaker of the language assigns to them, and this specification is made on the basis of the speaker's assent to and dissent from the sentences in the presence and the absence of certain circumstances respectively. The speaker's assent and dissent is the starting point of such a meaning theory. But the interpreter cannot specify the truth condition for a given sentence of the language for which a meaning theory is to be developed just on the basis of the fact that the speaker holds the sentence true in the presence of a certain situation, and she does not hold it true in the absence of it. The interpreter has also to know what the speaker believes the situation to be, and what her intentions are. The competent speaker's holding a sentence true in a certain situation is a function of at least three arguments — belief, meaning and intention. Even if we keep intention aside by ascribing the principle of honesty to the speaker we have to admit that the native speaker's holding a sentence true in a certain situation is a function of two arguments — belief and meaning. If we could know beforehand what the competent speaker believes the situation to be then on the basis of his holding the sentence true, we could also know what truth condition (meaning) she attaches to the sentence. Similarly, if we could know beforehand the meaning the speaker attaches to the sentence, then we could also know the belief of the speaker on the basis of his assent. But neither of them can be known independently of the other.

The Principle of Charity as a Solution to the Problem of Belief–Meaning Interlocking

Thus the problem is this: we suppose that we know that the speaker holds a given sentence true in a certain situation, and we want to know what she believes and what she means, where belief and meaning are interlocked. How to solve this impasse? Davidson's solution to this impasse conforms to the solution, given in the Bayesian theory developed by Ramsey and subsequently modified by Jeffrey, to the decision problem in probability theory. To solve the impasse in meaning theory Davidson appeals to the principle of charity. He holds that the interpreter should assume that the competent speaker believes the situation to be the same as believed by the interpreter. On the basis of this assumption the interpreter can move forward for specifying the truth conditions of the given sentence. In this way we can assign truth conditions to the sentences of the language.

Coherence as the Justification for a Davidsonian Meaning Theory

So far we have seen that according to Davidson, we can develop a meaning theory for a given language on the basis of the competent speaker's assent/dissent and the principle of charity. Such a theory specifies a *T*-sentence for every sentence of the language. But such a theory specifies a *T*-sentence for every sentence of the language. But such a theory cannot be elevated to an empirical theory unless it is verified as correct. An empirical theory is said to be correct if and only if its deliverances (theorems) are true. The theorems of a Davidsonian meaning theory for a language are the *T*-sentences for the sentences of the language yielded by the meaning theory. So if a truth conditional meaning theory is to be verified as correct it has to be established that the *T*-sentences yielded by the meaning theory are true. How can this be established? Here Davidson introduces his coherence theory of truth and knowledge. The essence of what he says is that a belief is associated with each *T*-sentence yielded by a meaning theory for a language. The belief associated with the *T*-sentence of a language can be taken as true, and so the *T*-sentence can also be taken as true, if the belief coheres with other beliefs associated with other sentences of the language. Here "coherence" means consistency. So a belief associated with a *T*-sentence, and also the *T*-sentence itself, can be established as true if the belief belongs to a mutually consistent set of beliefs associated with the *T*-sentences specified for the sentences of a given language by a Davidsonian meaning theory. Thus we see that according to Davidson, the meaning of a sentence of a language consists in the truth condition specified by the *T*-sentence yielded by a truth conditional meaning theory for the language. So to have understanding of a language is to possess a truth conditional meaning theory for the language. A person's understanding of a language is correct if the web of beliefs associated with the *T*-sentences for the sentences belonging to the language constitutes a mutually consistent set. Davidson says: "Each speaker can do or better than make this system of beliefs coherent adjusting the system as rationally as he can as new beliefs are thrust on him."[9]

Dummett's Critique of the Davidson Theory of Meaning

Dummett tries to prove the untenability of the Davidsonian theory of meaning with the help of the following reduction: First he takes as a premiss, the truth of which is established separately, that if the Davidsonian theory of meaning is admitted then we have to say that knowledge of meaning of a sentence implies our ability to recognize that the truth condition of it has obtained when it has so obtained. The second premiss of the argument is that we know the meaning of undecidable sentences. Therefore, it follows that we have the ability to recognize that the truth condition of an undecidable sentence has obtained when it has so obtained. But undecidable sentences are, ex-hypothesis, such that we cannot recognize that their truth conditions have obtained when they have obtained. Since we cannot do so we have to admit that we do not know the truth conditions (meanings) of undecidable sentences. This leads to a contradiction that we know and don't know the meaning of undecidable sentences.[10] In order to establish the truth of the first premiss Dummett argues that knowledge of the truth condition of a sentence must be implicit, otherwise an infinite regress or circularity will arise. Dummett explains this problem in the following manner. Knowledge may in principle be either explicit or implicit. Knowledge is explicit when the person can state what she knows, i.e. when she can assert some sentences that express the content of her knowledge. Then, of course, it is

---

9 Donald Davidson, 1986b, "Empirical Content".

10 Dummett, 1984, "What is a Theory of Meaning? (II)".

implied that she knows the meaning (truth condition) of the sentences that she asserts. The claim that a person knows something cannot be sustained unless the person is able to manifest this knowledge. Thus if the knowledge of truth condition of a sentence S_1 is claimed to be explicit then the person who knows the truth condition must be able to state the truth condition. Now in order to state the truth condition of S_1 the person has to know the truth conditions of the sentences S_1–S_n by the use of which the truth condition of S_1 is stated. Then the question of manifesting the person's knowledge of truth conditions of S_2–S_n will arise. If it is said to be manifested by stating their truth conditions in terms of some other sentences then the question of manifesting the truth conditions of those other sentences will arise, and in this way an infinite regress will arise. In order to avoid this infinite regress one may, at one point, resort to some sentence the truth condition of which is already stated. This recourse to some sentence the truth condition of which is already stated may avoid the above infinite regress but it will lead no circularity. So the knowledge of truth condition of a sentence cannot be explicit. The knowledge of truth condition of a sentence must, therefore, be implicit.

As ascription of implicit knowledge must always be explainable in terms of what counts as a manifestation of that knowledge, i.e. of some practical ability. Now if a person has a practical ability in knowing the truth condition (meaning) of a sentence, the manifestation of that ability must consist in deciding that the truth condition of that sentence has obtained when it has obtained. If a person cannot decide that the truth condition of a sentence has obtained when it has obtained then the person cannot obviously be said to have knowledge of truth condition of that sentence.

Now let us consider an undecidable sentence. Let us take the sentence uttered by a friend of Jones after he passed away, viz. "Jones was brave", where Jones lived a sheltered life, i.e. a life having no chance of showing his bravery. It is not possible in this case to decide whether the utterance made by Jones' friend is true even if the sentence is true, i.e. the truth condition of the sentence obtains, although we have knowledge of the meaning of the above sentence. So it is illegitimate to claim that what we know in knowing the meaning of the sentence is its truth condition. Thus Dummett argues that the Davidsonian truth condition theory of meaning cannot account for our understanding of undecidable sentence, and since a satisfactory theory of meaning is supposed to account for our understanding of all sentences of the concerned language the Davidsonian theory of meaning is not acceptable.

A Davidsonian Reply to the Dummettian Critique

What Dummett intends to say through his critique is that the Tarskian realistic truth theory cannot be the right theory for a language because the Davidsonian meaning theory, based on it, for a language cannot be regarded as a satisfactory theory of understanding, if the language involves undecidable sentences.

The assumption behind this problem is that the only legitimate way of manifesting our knowledge of meaning (truth condition) of a sentence is to decide that the truth condition has obtained as and when it has obtained. But this assumption is wrong. In the Davidsonian framework the manifestation of knowledge must be different. Davidson agrees with Dummett that the learner's knowledge of truth condition of a sentence must be implicit rather than explicit. It is a capacity, a dispositional knowledge. This capacity is manifested in doing something in appropriate situation. But Davidson would differ from Dummett over the issue of what constitutes this doing in appropriate situation. Dummett says that it is constituted by deciding that the sentence, the meaning of which is known, is true as and when it is true. The Davidsonian theory of meaning suggests that if an interpreter knows the meaning of a sentence then he can put the belief associated with the *T*-sentence for the sentence that specifies its truth condition in the holistic web of mutually supporting beliefs associated with the *T*-sentences specifying truth conditions of other sentences derived from the meaning theory for the language under consideration. In other words, he can relate the truth condition of it with the truth conditions of all other sentences of the language.

The competent speaker of a language who knows the truth condition (meaning) of an undecidable sentence can relate the truth condition of it with the truth conditions of other sentences of the language, and by doing that she manifests her knowledge of meaning of the undecidable sentence.

Dummett's charge against the Davidsonian theory of meaning is rooted in his belief that the only legitimate way of manifesting one's knowledge of truth condition (meaning) of a sentence is through deciding that the truth condition of the sentence obtains, as and when it obtains. I have shown that this is not the only legitimate way of manifesting one's knowledge of meaning of a sentence. Moreover the Dummettian suggestion regarding the way of manifesting one's knowledge of truth condition is illegitimate. Because having an implicit knowledge of the truth condition of a sentence is one thing and having the ability to decide whether the truth condition obtains is another. The former constitutes the dispositional knowledge of the competent speaker of the language, whereas the latter relates to her knowledge of truth of the sentence. Knowledge of truth condition and knowledge of truth are different things. One can have the former ability without having the latter, although one cannot have the latter ability without having the former.

Thus we see that the Davidsonian theory of meaning is holistic in nature. The Dummettian argument against the Davidsonian theory of meaning fizzles out if this is kept in mind. But this solution depends upon the legitimacy of holism, which is a big issue and required a separate in-depth study. Dummett, Fodor and many other philosophers have tried to refute holism. Bilgrami has given a reply to Dummett's critique of Davidson's holism. He has rightly argued that Dummett has not been able to come up with a critique of Davidson's holism which is independent of the truth theoretic conception of meaning.[11] I have given a reply to Fodor's critique of holism by showing that his critique is based on wrong conception of holism.[12] A similar controversy between

[11] Bilgrami, Akeel, 1986, "Meaning, Holism and Use".

[12] Chakraborti, Sadhan, 1998, "Semantic Holism verus Intentional Realism".

holism and anti-holism is found in Indian tradition between the Naiyāyikas and Bhartṛhari. J.L. Shaw and Hiranmoy Banerjee have made a comparative study of this issue.[13]

[13] Shaw, 2000, "Conditions for Understanding the Meaning of a Sentence"; Banerjee, 1997, "Bhartrihari".

10

Language, Communication and Miscommunication

HUMAN beings use language primarily for communication. All normal human beings want to be understood by others, at least by significant others, and for this purpose they use language. From the evolutionary perspective communication is an integral part of our life. It makes our survival and growth possible. Human communication has got two signalling systems — verbal (or written) and non-verbal — each of which contributes to what we communicate. When a person *A* (the speaker) uses a verbal language with a view to be understood by another person *B* (the hearer), *B* may try to understand *A* or *B* may not do so. If *B* tries to understand *A*, s/he may succeed in understanding *A* (at least to some extent) or s/he may fail to understand *A*. *B*'s failure usually brings in frustration in *B* as well as in *A*. But *B*'s success elicits positive feelings in *A* with a hope to have desirable reply from *B*. Cooperation from fellow beings that is essential for the survival and growth of a person is preceded by the person's communication to the fellow beings. A person can have cooperation from the fellow beings only if the person is understood by them. So communication has a great survival value, being understood by other is of immense importance to human beings. We also resort to non-verbal means with a view to being understood by others. Success or failure in understanding a person when the person uses verbal or non-verbal languange depends upon the fulfilment or non-fulfilment respectively of certain conditions. Philosophers, have engaged themselves in the study of these conditions, a study that is extremely important from the evolutionary perspective. The understanding of a person vis-à-vis language has got different aspects. One might succeed in understanding a person when the person uses a language in one aspect but fails to understand the person in another aspect. A comprehensive study of the conditions, the fulfilment of which leads to the success in understanding a person in different aspects, can help us not only in our everyday life but also in every field of interpersonal transaction. This paper reflects on the aspect of understanding a person vis-à-vis language and on the conditions associated with the different aspects the fulfilment of which makes the understanding possible.

First Aspect of Understanding

When a person uses a language with an intention to covey or express something to another person, the other person can understand him/her only if s/he knows the language used by the language user. Knowledge of language is a necessary condition for understanding a person on the basis of his/her use of language. One can understand what is said by a person by the use of a language only if one knows the meaning of the language. Understanding what is said by a person by the use of a language is the first aspect of understanding a person. Having knowledge of meaning of the concerned language is a necessary condition for this first aspect of understanding. Many deep philosophical issues are raised concerning knowledge of meaning. Some of the questions regarding knowledge of meaning which are addressed by philosophers over a long time are: What constitutes our knowledge of meaning of a language? How is this knowledge obtained? Is knowing of this kind knowing that or knowing how or knowing what? Is knowledge of meaning innate or acquired? Different philosophical views are found in the literature over these issues. The Davidsonian theory appears to give satisfactory answers to some of these questions.

Davidson's Pro-theory Approach

I have said in the previous chapter that in philosophy of language the various approaches to meaning can broadly be classified into

(a) pro-theory approach, and (b) anti-theory approach. Later Wittgenstein's approach to meaning, for example, is anti-theory approach, whereas Chomsky's approach to meaning is pro-theory approach. Later Wittgenstein[1] does not admit that a competent speaker of a language possesses a meaning theory. By contrast Chomsky[2] admits a species specific Language Acquisition Device (LAD) in a human being by the use of which a speaker of a language develops a meaning theory for the language when s/he learns it. Davidson's approach to meaning belongs to the latter kind. Behaviourists characterize understanding of language in terms of behaviour-linguistic and non-linguistic. Davidson holds that characterizing understanding of language in terms of linguistic and non-linguistic behaviour is inadequate. Davidson adheres to Searle's famous "Chinese Room Argument".[3] A speaker of a language can have a capacity to exhibit appropriate linguistic and non-linguistic behaviour without having any understanding of the language under consideration. Davidson also adheres to Chomsky's "Poverty of Stimulus Argument".[4] The behaviouristic theory cannot account for the creativity of a language user. Within a short period of time a speaker of a language can generate many sentences and use them appropriately although she has never come across the use of those sentences. According to Davidson, understanding of a language consists in the possession of a meaning theory for that language.

Davidson proposes that the study of meaning is best approached via theories of meaning. In the early 1960s, the philosophy of language was radically altered when Davidson redefined both what form a meaning theory for a natural language can take and what condition of adequacy, both empirical and formal, such theories should meet. Along with Quine, he discouraged philosophers from analysing such individual concepts

---

1 Wittgenstein, 1958, *Philosophical Investigations*.

2 Chomsky, 1980, *Rules and Representation*.

3 Searle, 1980, "Minds, Brains and Programs".

4 Chomsky, 1964, "A Review of B.F. Skinner's Verbal Behaviour".

as meaning. Instead, he framed questions about meaning theory in the context of understanding language. In this context he draws a distinction between theory of meaning and meaning theory. The kind of theory a philosopher of language advocates is called by him "theory of meaning", and the kind of theory a field linguist is concerned with is called by him "meaning theory". A meaning theory is concerned with a specific language, whereas a philosopher aims at developing a theory of meaning that specifies what meaning theories for specific languages lay bare. So a philosopher's theory of meaning, which, according to Davidson, is a theory of understanding, is a second order theory.

Dummett, and Davidson as well, would make a distinction in this context between a truth theory and a meaning theory for a language. A truth theory specifies truth conditions for the sentences of a language, whereas a meaning theory gives an account of the understanding of the language. The truth theory and the meaning theory for a language are closely related although they are different. Dummett observes that the former constitutes the base of the latter.[5] A proposed truth theory for a language can be justified if a satisfactory meaning theory for the language can be constructed on the basis of it.

Please keep in mind what is said in the previous chapter about Davidson's truth-theoretic account of understanding of language.

We see that the first aspect of understanding vis-à-vis language used by a competent speaker, i.e. the understanding of what is said by the speaker, requires knowledge or understanding of the language, which consists in having a correct meaning theory for the language. Truth condition theorists hold that such a meaning theory consists in a theory of truth conditions for the sentences belonging to the language.

Second Aspect of Understanding

The first aspect of understanding is the aspect of understanding what is said. Understanding a user of a language by means of

5 Dummett, 1991, *The Logical Basis of Metaphysics.*

understanding what is said is only a stepping stone toward understanding the mind of the competent speaker. This aspect of understanding helps one to arrive at a deeper aspect of understanding — the aspect of understanding what is meant. The distinction between what is said and what is meant in communication by the use of language was stressed by Paul Grice.[6] Let us explain this distinction with the help of an example. Suppose in a selection committee professor *A* asks another professor *B*, a professor of philosophy, for an evaluation of his student Mr *X*. Accordingly *B* utters the sentence *S*: "Mr *X* has excellent handwriting and is always very punctual". From this utterance the members of the selection committee understand what is meant by *B*: they conclude that *B* thinks that Mr *X* is not much good in philosophy. It is evident that what is said (the literal meaning of the sentence *S*) and what is meant by the use of *S* are different. The semantic apparatus cannot bridge the gap between what is said and what is meant by the use of *S*. Another apparatus required for arriving at what is meant from what is said is called by Grice "the pragmatic apparatus". The second aspect understanding, i.e. the aspect of understanding what is meant by the use of a language, can be accounted for with the help of this apparatus.

The Pragmatic Apparatus

The pragmatic apparatus consists of certain pragmatic principles and we achieve the second aspect of understanding on the basis of these principles. The overarching principle of this apparatus is the cooperative principle, which can be formulated in the following way:

> Make your conversational contribution such as is required, at the stage at which it is required, by the accepted purpose or direction of the talk exchange in which you are engaged.

There are four categories of specific maxims, and sub-maxims under these maxims, subsumed under this principle. These are:

---

[6] Grice, 1989, *Studies in the Way of Words*.

Quantity: Make your contribution as informative, as is required (for the current purposes of exchange); do not make your contribution more informative than is required.

Quality: Try to make your contribution one that is true. Specifically: (1) Do not say what you believe to be false; (2) Do not say that for which you lack adequate evidence.

Relation: Be relevant.

Manner: Be perspicuous. Specifically: (1) be brief; (2) be orderly; (3) avoid ambiguity; and (4) avoid obscurity of expression.

Grice's basic idea is that there is a systematic correspondence between what a competent speaker means and the assumptions required in order to preserve the supposition that s/he is observing the cooperative principle and conversational maxims. In the case of professor *B*'s evaluation of Mr *X* if we do not go beyond what is said by *B* there occurs an intentional and overt violation of the cooperative principle or of one or more of the maxims. If *B* does not mean something different from what is said by uttering *S*: "Mr X has excellent handwriting and is always very punctual" in the context mentioned earlier then *B* seems to have violated one of the maxims of quantity or the maxim of relation. If Mr *X* is one of *B*'s students then *B* must be in a position to volunteer more relevant information than information about Mr *X*'s handwriting and timekeeping. Furthermore *B* knows that more information is required. The members of the selection committee are naturally led to the conclusion that *B* is trying to convey something different from what is said by the use of *S*, something more relevant to the purposes at hand. In the mentioned context had *B* thought that Mr *X* was any good in philosophy he would have said so. Therefore it transpires that *B* thinks that Mr *X* is not good in philosophy and is unwilling to say so. Thus the members of the selection committee understand that what *B* means by the use of *S* is that Mr *X* is not good in philosophy. It is evident from this example that what a competent speaker means by the use of a language cannot be understood with the help of the semantic apparatus if what s/he means is different from what is said by the use of it. Mere knowledge of the literal meaning of an expression of a language uttered by a speaker does not suffice to understand what is meant by the use of it. The hearer's knowledge of the pragmatic principles also plays a significant role in understanding what is meant by the competent speaker by means of using a language. Thus the second aspect of understanding, i.e. the aspect of understanding what is said requires knowledge not only of the semantic apparatus but also of the pragmatic apparatus.

Third Aspect of Understanding

The third aspect of understanding of a user of a language is the aspect of understanding what is felt by the user. While doing philosophy of language, philosophers are usually concerned with the propositional content of language and not with the felt part, which is also an important part of the content of language. They sometimes go to the extent of that part of mind, which is constituted by beliefs, but the part of mind, which is constituted by our emotions, usually remains untouched in philosophical discourse. Some philosophers are of course concerned with the language of emotions, but what they are really concerned with is the content of this language, not the felt part of the user of a language that s/he intends to communicate. A competent speaker of a language intends to communicate not only the prepositional content, i.e. what is said, or what is meant by the speaker by the use of an expression of the language, she also intends to communicate certain emotion/s; and for this s/he need not use any emotion term. S/he can attempt to communicate his/her emotions through non-verbal expressions or verbal intonations or modulation of speech. Understanding a user of a language cannot be complete unless the emotions associated with his/her use of language is understood along with what is said or what is meant by him/her. Lack of understanding of the felt part leads to miscommunication.

A Case Excerpt

Let me present a brief excerpt of a case dealt with by a psychotherapist and explain how miscommunication takes place in the absence of the understanding of the felt part. This is a case of a couple. Koushik and Piu got married eight years back. Both of them are school teachers. Koushik performs his family duties with sincerity but at his core he is a thoughtful person with keen interest in intellectual activities. He has published some books and articles, which have been appreciated by intellectuals. He has varied interests and actively participates in seminars and workshops on different themes. Koushik is also very sociable, helpful and friendly, and he is widely connected to people from different walks of life. He engages himself in social works, especially in the service of those who are marginalized in our society. Piu, on the other hand, is a docile lady mostly concerned with her school and household matters with less interest in academics and social work. Piu comes to the psychotherapist with the complaints that her husband does not spend even minimum time with her; recently he has stopped talking to her, he has been sleeping in a separate room and Piu is suspecting that Koushik has developed illicit relationships. Piu, very angry and confused both intellectually and behaviourally, expresses that she was being deprived of her right to have sufficient time from her husband and the right to have her husband as her bed-partner. She is totally shattered to think that her husband has developed illicit relationship.

After a few sessions with the couple, focusing mainly on their communication pattern and behavioural modification, it is revealed that there are huge gaps between the intellectual and emotional aspects of Koushik and Piu. Koushik enjoys being involved in high intellectual thinking but Piu is seldom interested in it. Emotionally Koushik is not only romantic, he wants to love his wife deeply and also wants to be loved by her, whereas Piu rarely expresses her romance and her aspect of love is very shallow. The value systems of Koushik and Piu are also very different. Dignity, intellectual exercise, deep love, good interpersonal relationship and cooperation are some of the prime values, which constitute Koushik's value system, but most of these are not among the priorities of Piu. Frequent verbal abuse and constant assault on the value system of Koushik by Piu has made him irritated, frustrated and gradually it has led to Koushik's detachment from Piu. He is now totally withdrawn from Piu and sleeps in a separate room. This has perturbed Piu. Piu's self-esteem is very low and as a result of it she has developed delusion of infidelity: Piu cannot respect and love herself deeply and so she has failed to respect and love Koushik and to be loved by Koushik in his cherished sense of love.

Regarding the issue of Piu's right to have adequate time from Koushik the psychotherapist has discussed with the couple at length, and an in-depth analysis of their spending time for themselves through participating in dialogues at different occasions has shown that in most of the occasions they had very unhappy endings due to the differences they have as mentioned above. The time they devoted for themselves decreased their quality of life. So as a survival strategy Koushik has stopped giving time to his wife.

The social dimension of the problem has doubled the trouble of the couple. Despite financial security Piu is not ready to go for divorce even though she feels that it is impossible for her to live with dignity with Koushik as her husband. She is afraid of the blaming she is anxious of having from the patriarchal society she lives in. People would accuse her only for their divorce; they will constantly point their fingers at her and try to devalue her, which is very difficult for Piu to cope with. In fact, it is difficult even for those women whose self-esteem is not very low. They would not consider the fact that these two individuals are very different in many respects; very few people of our society have learned to use the bio–psycho–social model for looking at an individual. Most of them are yet to recognize that an individual has three dimensions — biological, psychological and social. They fail to perceive that the biological constitutions and the mental make-ups of Koushik and Piu are very different; that they are brought up in different social situations and in different manners, their life events are also very different; so they have imbibed different value systems and belief systems; their emotional patterns were also very different; and that these differences are responsible for their miscommunication.

Piu, however, failed to understand the felt aspect of Koushik involved in what he intended to communicate by his utterances along with other non-verbal and behavioural expressions during their dialogue. Koushik expressed his feeling of love through verbal and non-verbal expressions, but Piu failed to grasp it although she succeeded in understanding in most cases what is said and what is meant by Koushik. As a result the kind of verbal and non-verbal feedback of Piu frustrated Koushik. This failure of communication of what is felt, which is different from what is said and what is meant, by the use of verbal and non-verbal language deprived them of developing a fulfilling and adaptive relationship, instead it led to severe depression on the part of Koushik, and restlessness on the part of Piu. It hindered their growth or development and their survival is at stake.

The root cause of this unfortunate result due to miscommunication is the divergence in many respects of their personalities: their likes/dislikes, interests, beliefs, needs, desires, emotions, values and personal constructs. As Piu had a sense of love that was different from the sense in which Koushik understood it, Piu thought that she loved Koushik very much but Koushik was not satisfied with it at all. Different personal constructs of love operating in them led to miscommunication between Piu and Koushik.

From the evolutionary perspective miscommunication has a strong negative value. It leads to unhealthy or maladaptive relationship. Miscommunication may take place in any of the three aspects of understanding, viz., the aspects of what is said, what is meant and what is felt, but the probability of miscommunication at the third aspect, i.e. in the aspect of what is felt is much higher than its probability in other two aspects of understanding. Understanding what is felt in any case of communication in any field of our life is extremely important. The more we can understand the emotions associated with the use of language the more fulfilling relationship can we develop and so we can achieve more growth or development. Besides understanding what is felt, giving appropriate feedback relating to emotions understood either verbally or non-verbally is also necessary for developing satisfying relationship.

Feeling and Emotion

What is feeling? How is it related to behavioural expression on the basis of which we ascribe feeling to a person? These are special issues under the general problem of other minds. An account of the understanding of the felt part in communication involves a characterization of feeling and an explanation of the relation between observation of behavioural expression and understanding (or ascription) of feeling. Neurologists distinguish between feeling and emotion. They hold that emotion is a neurological state but feeling is a subjective experience arising out of a neurological state of emotion. Some specific connections between certain parts of out brain are responsible for our feeling. If these connections are cut off then our feeling stops, which we used to have before the connections were cut off. If certain connections between the amygdala and the hippocampus of a person were destroyed then the person would know intellectually to be afraid but s/he would not feel afraid as she used to do before the connections were destroyed.

Philosophers differ in characterizing feeling. I am not going to discuss different characterizations offered by different philosophers here. My characterization of feeling is an extension of the characterization given by William James. According to James,[7] feeling is the emotional experience of bodily changes. I think the concept of feeling is a cluster concept. The phenomenon of feeling involves specific neural pattern in the brain, cognitive awareness arising out of the pattern, emotional experience arising

[7] James, 1890, *Principles of Psychology*.

out of the pattern, verbal and non-verbal manifestations of the emotional experience and the range of possible activities. A feeling or emotional experience cannot be characterized without these other factors.

The Kinesic Apparatus

How can we understand emotions involved in communication? Some of those who study non-verbal behaviour communicating emotion (kinesics) claim that there are universal facial (and other bodily) expressions of emotions. Thinkers like Darwin, Eibl-Eibesfeldt, Izard and Tornkins uphold this view. On the other hand, Birdwhistell, LaBarre, Leach and Mead are among those who claim cultural variance in the facial (and other bodily) expressions of emotion. Paul Ekman resolves this issue by pointing out that although both of these warring groups are concerned with facial activities, they are not concerned with the same kind of facial activities. The relativists describe the cultural variations in the non-emotional facial activities and they confuse these with the facial universals in emotional expression. Conversely, the universalists focus on the emotional facial expressions and do not distinguish them from facial activities that are unrelated to emotion. Ekman makes his position clear by giving an account of the kinesic apparatus operative in communication.

Ekman's Neurocultural Account of Emotion

Universalists' characterization of emotion is biological, whereas relativists' characterization is sociocultural. By contrast, Ekman emphasizes biological and sociocultural determinants of emotion. He claims that the kinesic apparatus, the knowledge of which helps understanding emotions, consists of certain internal mechanisms — (a) an affect programme, (b) an appraisal system, (c) elicitors, (d) display rules, and (e) coping mechanism. Our non-verbal behaviour, i.e. manifestation of emotion or[8] emotional response is governed by this apparatus. Emotional responses are

[8] Ekman, 1980, "Biological and Cultural Contribution to Body and Facial Movement in the Expression of Emotion".

brief, often quick, complex, organized and difficult to control. The term "affect programme" refers to a mechanism that stores the patterns for these complex organized responses, and which when set off directs their occurrence. The organization of emotional response systems dictated by the affect programme has a genetic basis but is influenced also by experience. Behind the affect programme there is an internal mechanism, which Ekman calls an appraisal system that activates the affect programme into operation. This system selectively attends to those stimuli (external or internal) which are the occasion for activating the affect programme and operates automatically. It quickly attends to certain stimuli, determining not only that they pertain to emotion but to which emotion and then activating the appropriate part of the affect programme. When the automatic appraiser responds to a stimulus, setting off the affect programme that directs a particular complex, organized set of emotional responses, appraisal does not necessarily stop. The event may continue to unfold, new stimuli may be emitted, which again are subject to automatic appraisal → affect programme → emotional responses. The same emotion may be repeatedly triggered, or a number of different emotions may be triggered sequentially or simultaneously.

The term elicitor refers only to those stimuli that are identified by the automatic appraiser as specific for one or another emotion. The connection between specific stimulus and an emotional response is neither given nor fixed. Probably there is no emotion for which there is a universal elicitor, and there is no elicitor that always calls forth the same uninterruptible set of emotional responses. Cultural anthropology is replete with accounts of great variety in the specifics of what elicits one or another emotion. Most of the specific elicitors for emotion are variable, learned through different experiences. From a disgust facial expression (nose wrinkled, upper lips raised, etc.) of a person one cannot know what made the person disgusted; it depends upon his/her personal experiences. What is disgusting varies within as well as between cultures. While the specific elicitors for emotion vary with individual experience, there is also some commonality apparent in the general outline of what elicits the emotions through automatic appraisal and affect programme. Disgust elicitors share the characteristics of being noxious rather than painful; and in all cultures taste stimuli are among the elicitors of disgust. Surprise elicitors share the characteristics of being unexpected, novel and usually sudden rather than gradual. Fear elicitors share the characteristic of portending harm or pain. One of the common characteristics of some of the elicitors of happiness is release from accumulated pressure, tension, discomfort and the like. Loss of something to which one is intimately attached might be a common characteristic of sadness elicitors. Interference with ongoing activity might be characteristic of some anger elicitors. Elicitors for each emotion share some characteristics. The automatic appraiser is sensitive to these general characteristics.

When an elicitor is automatically appraised, the affect programme is set off, and organized complex emotional responses begin interference is still possible. The emotional responses may be interrupted, diminished, amplified, or masked with the appearance of another emotion. The phrase "display rule" refers to the conventions, norms and habits that develop regarding the management of emotional responses. A display rule specifies who can show what emotion to whom and when. These rules are learned so well that they typically operate automatically. For example, the prohibition against showing anger, or the rule to substitute sadness for anger, is learned so well by some middle-class American girls, that later, if liberated, it requires a lot of struggle to get their anger out. There are also personal display rules, which do not reflect cultural norms, but a more individualized experience. The management of emotional responses may occur also by deliberate choice of the moment, for a particular advantage, rather than as part of a long-standing personal or cultural display rule. Sometimes the emotional responses escape attempts to conceal them. This is called "leakage". When the management is deliberate, it is likely that some of the emotional response systems governed by the affect programme may be noticeable at least briefly, unless the person was alerted ahead of time and prepared himself/herself.

"Coping" refers to attempts to deal with the emotion felt and its source; to increase, diminish, or sustain what is occurring. Coping includes various cognitive activities as well as such organized behaviour as fight or flight. We discover how to cope with our emotions, what is likely to be successful, proper or improper. Once coping techniques have been acquired, they can become so well learned that they operate automatically and are called forth when the affect programme is set off.

All these components — the appraisal system, the affect programme, elicitors, display rules and coping mechanism — together constitute the kinesic apparatus operative in emotional expression. Thus knowledge of the functioning of this apparatus is necessary for understanding what is felt by a user of a language.

In addition to the knowledge of the functioning of the kinesic apparatus one has also to have subjective experience of an emotion in combination with other factors associated with it in order to understand similar emotional experience or feeling. One cannot fully understand another person's feeling of fear unless one has oneself experienced it. Absence of subjective experience on the part of the hearer of an emotion involved in a dialogue is one of the sources of miscommunication.

Therefore understanding a person comprehensively vis-à-vis use of language requires knowledge of the functioning of the kinesic apparatus and subjective experience of the concerned emotion as well as that of the semantic apparatus and the pragmatic apparatus. I agree with Buck and VanLear[9] that a general theory of communication must accommodate the relationship between verbal and non-verbal communication. What I like to add to this view is that such a theory of communication must accommodate all the three aspects — what is said, what is meant and what is felt — involved in communication.

---

9 Ross Buck and C. Arthur VanLear, 2002, "Verbal and Non-verbal Communication".

11

Representation, Meaning and Truth

THE divide between inferential role semantics and truth conditional semantics in philosophy of language has been revitalized by Robert Brandom's forceful attempt to defend inferentialism[1] considering it as opposed to representationalism. Putting Brandom's inferentialism kind of philosophical view aside we can say that philosophy of language in the West is concerned with three broad questions:

1. What is the relationship between language and the world?
2. What is the relationship between our mind and the world?
3. What is the relationship between our language and our mind?

In the context of the first question it is commonly said that speakers use language to describe how the world is. Typically, the use of language to describe the world is glossed by saying that language is a type of *representation,* and that words or sentences stand for the world (or chunks of it). The word "parrot", for example, can represent a particular red-beaked bird and the sentence "that parrot can speak" can represent the fact that the bird in question can speak. The philosophical question that has bothered philosophers is how is it possible for language to represent the world?

Representationalism in philosophy of language has a long tradition. Many philosophers before the twentieth century held that mental images form the basis of the power of language to

---

[1] Brandom: (a) 2000, *Articulating Reasons: An Introduction to Inferentialism;* (b) 2007, "Inferentialism and Some of Its Challenges".

present things. Hume,[2] for example, explicitly identified ideas as images and observed that language represents the world through ideas associated with it. In the beginning of twentieth century Bertrand Russell wrote:

> We must attach some meaning to the words we use, if we are to speak significantly and not utter mere noise; and the meaning we attach to our words must be something with which we are acquainted.[3]

According to Russell, we are confronted with things (entities) and somehow make our words stand for them. Representing or ending for things in the world makes our words meaningful. Many philosophers of the twentieth century took some form of presentationalism for granted. Wittgenstein's earlier theory in *Trctatus*,[4] Etchemendy's[5] representational semantics, Fodor's[6] notion of semantics as an annex to his representational theory of mind, Devitt's[7] semantics based on the concept of reference are taken to be some of the examples of the twentieth-century resentationalism in philosophy of language.

The second question, i.e. the question regarding the relationship between mind and world, or thought and world is seen to be answered in two different ways. Some philosophers contend that our mind represents the world through images. This view can be traced back to the classical Greek philosophy. Aristotle,[8] for example, said, "The soul never thinks without a mental image". This view was almost universally accepted in the philosophical tradition from the Greek philosophy uptil the emergence of twentieth-century philosophy. Of course, there are some

---

[2] Hume, 1967, *An Enquiry Concerning Human Understanding*.

[3] Russell, 1912, *The Problems of Philosophy*.

[4] Wittgenstein, 1961b, *Tractatus Logico-Philosophicus*.

[5] Etchemendy, 1990, *The Concept of Logical Consequence*.

[6] Fodor: (a) 1981, *Representations*; (b) 1998, *Concepts*.

[7] M. Devitt, 1991, "The Methodology of Naturalistic Semantics".

[8] Aristotle, *De Anima*, 431a, 15-20.

dissenting voices, e.g. the voices of Gilbert Ryle,[9] Ludwig Wittgenstein, Moritz Schlick and Jean-Paul Sartre,[10] which contributed to the decline of interest in imagery in both, analytical and phenomenological tradition. Although imagery lost its earlier glory in the twentieth century, a significant number of philosophers continued admitting image-like entities through which our mind was claimed to represent the world. After the rise of cognitive science this was prominent. In cognitive science, cognition is viewed as a computational manipulation of symbols expressed in mentalese — language of thought. Fodor championed this view. S.M. Kosslyn[11] developed a quasi-pictorial computational theory of visual imagery. Description and quasi-pictorial theorists disagreed sharply over what sorts of computational symbols or data structures are acceptable within cognitive theory.

However, one thing that philosophers are not inclined to deny is ingeniously formulated by Franz Brentano[12] in characterizing the thought or the mental, viz. intentionality. According to him, mind or thought is intentional. It is directed towards objects. In characterizing the mental in terms of intentionality Brentano maintains neutrality regarding the nature of objects towards which our mind or thought is directed. Neither mental in existence nor real existence of things is committed in such characterization.

"Intentionality" is often used interchangeably with "representationality". "Mental states are intentional" is used to mean that mental states represent things towards which they are directed. Taken in this sense, an external realist who admits external objects and contends that mental states are directed towards external objects, may be said to hold a representationalist theory of mind. Now one may subscribe to the view that mental states are directed to the external objects not through any intermediary, entity like idea or imagery or entities having mental

---

9 Ryle, 1955, *The Concept of Mind.*

10 Sartre, 1962, *Imagination: A Psychological Critique.*

11 Kosslyn, 1983, *Ghosts in the Mind's Machine.*

12 Brentano, 1995, *Psychology from an Empirical Standpoint.*

in existence. One may hold that mental states are directly directed to the external objects. Philosophers advocating this view are called "naïve realists".

The above sense of "representationality" entitles inclusion of naïve realists in the camp of representationalists. The above exposition of representationality suggests that the content of a sentence, for both a naïve realist and a representative realist, is an external state of affairs. Both of them would adhere to the view that a sentence represents an external state of affairs. The only difference between them would be that a naïve realist would contend that a sentence represents, whatever it represents, directly, not through any intermediary, whereas a representationalist would hold that the external state of affairs is represented by a sentence through an intermediary.

A representative realist, who is also an external realist, upholds the view that our thoughts are directed towards external objects only through intermediaries constituted by ideas or imagery or similar entities. These are the direct (immediate) objects of our thought. External objects are thought of by us through our thinking of the immediate objects of our thoughts. If "representationality" is used interchangeably with "intentionality" then representative realists can also be called representationalists.

Even those who restrict our thoughts to be directed to internal entities, cannot be barred from being included in the camp of representationalists under the above interpretation of the term "representationality".

There is a similarity between representationality and intentionality. When we say that thought is intentional, what we intend to say is that thought is always a thought of something. This holds in the case of representationality too. "Our thoughts are representational" means our thoughts are thoughts of something. What can be disputed — is that representationality like intentionality consists in *being of something*. One may contend that apart from being of something representationality involves *indirectness*. On this view when we say our thoughts are representational in nature what we intend to say is (i) a thought is of something, and (ii) a thought provides a model of the thing of which it is a thought. So it is argued that intentionality is one of the components of representationality.

A representationalist would say about mind or thought in this sense that the content of our thought is a model of reality. The content of propositional attitude, for example, is a model of reality. *X*'s belief to the effect that Delhi is to the north of Kolkata is a depiction of the geographical relationship between Delhi and Kolkata. It is through this depiction (model) that *X*'s belief represents the geographical relationship between Delhi and Kolkata.

The theory of truth that is compatible with this kind of representationality thesis about thought characterizes truth in terms of correspondence. A representationalist would say that a belief is true if and only if the content of it corresponds to the reality of which the content is a model.

Regarding the question of the relationship between language and mind it is commonly held that speakers use language to express, more or less accurately, what they are thinking. If Sabina is thinking that children are playing merrily, she can say that. Here priority of thought over language is envisaged. Language is viewed as a vehicle of thought. Language represents the content of thought. Mental representation and linguistic representation are two ways of representing the same thing. The content in mental representation is the same as the content in linguistic representation. The content may be claimed to consist in the external situation or in some internal situation or in some existents or concepts.

The received opinion of our time is *that* linguistic representation is a derivative of mental representation. So emphasis is being given on the study of mental representation.

Of different forms of representationalism, mental or linguistic, these which aim at giving an account of how our language or word represents the empirical reality has always been fascinating philosophers. Those philosophical theories of mental/linguistic representation of empirical reality have drawn much attention of thinkers in this area which endorse the human predicament pointed out by Kant, viz. that our knowledge of external reality is possible only through our senses.

The cognitive neuroscientist's account of our mind representing the world endorsing the above human predicament is now believed to be the scientific account of it. Having an idea of the neuroscientist's account of our mind's representation of the world helps in engaging ourselves in a meaningful discussion about the philosophical issues centring linguistic/mental representationalism.

The neuroscientists' account of the neurological processes which generate perceptual experience gives an idea of their view of mind's representing the empirical world. Neuroscientists have given much emphasis on the visual system, because it is fairly similar in man and the higher primates and so appropriate experiments on such animals may be relevant to the study of neural mechanism underlying perceptual experience in humans; indeed 50 per cent of the cortex in the Macaque monkey is devoted to visual perception. Another reason why vision is so important is that it enables us to perceive information at a distance, to engage in remote sensing by which we can avoid a predator better — it is too late to flee once sharp teeth pierce the skin. If the neurological processes involved in visual perception are understood then it will be easier to understand the neurological processes involved in other modalities of perception.

Visual information is contained in the light reflected from an object. To perceive an object we need sensory receptors that respond to the reflected light. As light passes through the lens of the eye, the image is inverted and focused to project on the back surface of the eye, the retina comprises millions of photoreceptors, each containing light-sensitive molecules or photopigments. When exposed to light, the photopigments become unstable and split apart. Then decomposition alters the flow of the electrical current around the photoreceptors. This light-induced change triggers action potentials in downstream neurons. Then photoreceptors provide for translation from an external stimulus, light, into an internal neural signal, the detection of that stimulus.

Photoreceptors are of two types — rods and cones. Rods are sensitive to low-level stimulation and so useful at night when light energy is reduced. Cones require more intense levels of light and so they are active during daytime vision. Cones are essential for colour vision.

Extensive signal processing of visual information is performed within the retina. The output from the photoreceptors is first processed in the bipolar cells and from there in the ganglion cells. Extensive convergence of information happens within this processing layer of the retina. Axons of the ganglion cells form a bundle, the optic nerve. By way of this nerve, visual information is transmitted to the central nervous system. Within the brain each optic nerve divides into pathways that differ where they terminate within the subcortex. One such pathway starting from the retina reaches the Lateral Geniculate Nuclei (LGN) of the thalamus. This pathway contains more than 90 per cent of the axons in the optic nerve and provides input to the cortex. The remaining 10 per cent of the fibres innervate other subcortical structures including the pulvenar nucleus of the midbrain. The final projection to the visual cortex is via the geniculo-cortical pathway. This bundle of axons exits from LGN and ascends to the cortex, with almost all of the fibres terminating in primary visual area of the occipital lobe. Thus visual information in the cortex is processed by at least five distinct neurons: photoreceptors, bipolar cells, ganglion cells, LGN cells and cortical cells.

The strongest hypothesis in visual perception is that visual information is distributed across distinct subsystems. On this view perception is analytic. Early processes are devoted to analysing attributes of a stimulus: some processes represent shape, some other processes focus on colour, and the rest provide information about the dynamics or movement in the visual scene.

Distinct regions of visual processing are identified in the cortex like V_1, V_2, V_3, and V_4. Each visual area has a topographic representation of external space in the contralateral hemifield. An area is defined by a discontinuity in the retinotropic representation of the cells. Neurons within an area not only decode where an object is located in visual space, but also provide vivid information about the object's external attributes.

Visual perception is a divide-and-conquer strategy. Rather than each visual area representing all attributes of an object, each provides its own limited analysis. Processing is distributed and specialized. As we advance through the visual system, different areas elaborate on the initial information in V_1 and begin to integrate this information across dimensions to form recognizable percepts.

Neuroimaging studies {mainly based on functional Magnetic Resonance Imaging (fMRI) and Positron Emisson Tomography (PET)} have opened a new window for studying visual perception. The results of these studies suggest that perception involves higher visual areas rather than the primary visual cortex. Features like colour, shape and motion are processed along distinct neural pathways. But perception requires more than simply perceiving the features of objects. When we look at an object we perceive a unified object. Object recognition is more than linking features to trigger memories.

Failures of perception can occur even when processes, such as the analysis of colour, shape and motion, are intact. This disorder is limited to the visual modality. The syndrome is referred as visual agnosia. Neuroscientists have identified two pathways in higher visual areas, viz. the virtual or occipito-temporal pathway and the dorsal or occipito-parietal pathway. The former is specialized for object perception for determining what it is we are looking at and the latter is specialized for spatial perception, for determining where an object is, and for analysing the spatial configuration between different objects in a sense. "What" and "where" are the two basic questions in visual perception which are answered by these two pathways.[13] The neuroscientists appear to say that the external reality consists of waves and particles, which are imperceptible, but they are causally responsible for generating inner representations in the form of nerve signals the processing of which ultimately generates perceptual experience. Thus it seems that the neurophysical account of perception is a form of representationalism.

Representationalists generally make use of what is dubbed as "the argument from illusion" to show that direct realism is impossible, and that there must be sensory inputs that are directly (immediately) grasped by our perceptual experience. The argument from illusion may be formulated thus:

(a) Cases of perceptual illusion are facts.

(b) What we are immediately aware of in such an illusion are not the external objects but the sensory inputs the indubitability of which is guaranteed by the perceptual experience itself.

(c) In respect of epistemic status there is no difference between veridical perception and illusory perception.

(d) Therefore, like the objects of illusory experience objects of veridical perception are also sensory inputs, not external objects.

The argument from variability is also levelled by representationalists against direct realism. In spite of the object constancy we have different perceptual experiences at different moments as is the case with face-vase variability. So what we directly experience in perception cannot be the external object, it is rather our internal representation.

In neurophysical account, perception is explained as a modification of the brain that comprehends the specific nature of the external object. The external object is actually inferred from the internal representation of it.

---

[13] Gazzaniga, Ivry and Mangun, 2002, *Cognitive Neuroscience.*

One of the problems encountered by the upholders of the neurophysical theory of perception, who seem to be representationalists, is that if it is said that we infer the external objects on the basis of inner representations, where inner representations are taken to be caused by the waves and particles which constitute the external world then a direct knowledge of certain relation is to be admitted between inner representations and external objects (waves and particles). Now, in order to have this knowledge we must have knowledge of inner representations and external waves and particles separately. According to the neurophysical theory of perception inner representations are known directly but we do not have direct knowledge of the external waves and particles. It is difficult to account for how one can have inferential knowledge of waves and particles, which cause inner representations, on the basis of knowledge of inner representations.

Such an inferential knowledge could be admitted had the argument been a transcendetal one. The argument that this theory resorts to is rather a causal argument. Knowledge of causality between *A* and *B* requires independent knowledge of *A* and *B*.

If the neurophysical theory of perception is not treated as representationalism then it tantamounts to phenomenalism. Phenomenalists, unlike representationalists, do not claim to have inferential knowledge of external reality. They hold that what we perceive is our construction from the sensory inputs that we receive.

Some neuroscientists tend to view the neurophysical theory of perception as a form of phenomenalism. Semir Zeki, for example, quotes the following passage from Kant:

> All presentations have a necessary reference to a possible empirical consciousness, for if they did not have this reference, and becoming conscious of them were entirely impossible, then this would be tantamount to saying that they do not exist at all. But all empirical consciousnesses have a necessary reference to a transcendental consciousness (a consciousness that precedes

> all particular experience), viz. the consciousness of myself as original apperception.

Then he says:

> Here, I disagree only with the suggestion that the "empirical" (micro) consciousness has a necessary reference to the unified, transcendental consciousness.[14]

If the neurophysical account is taken as a form of phenomenalism then it has to admit like Kant, noumena (things-in-themselves) which consists of things unknown and unknowable, or the propounders of this theory have to sever the relationship of inner representations from external reality and thus conceding much to the sceptics.

If we do not deny or doubt the existence of external reality, if we are not idealists or sceptics, then the only option seems to be to admit that the external objects and events are perceived directly. Thus direct realism seems to be the only plausible view of our representation of the external world. But perhaps this goes against the neurophysical account of it.

Quine views the above neuro-scientific account of our experience of the empirical world as naturalism. It is a rational reconstruction of the individual's and/or the race's actual acquisition of a responsible theory of the external world. It would address the question how we, physical denizens of the physical world, can have projected our scientific theory of the world from our meagre contacts with it: from the mere impacts of rays and particles on our surfaces and a few odds and ends such as the strain of walking uphill.

The kind of naturalism Quine advocates takes, as a physical analogue of Carnap's elementary experience, *global stimulus* as the foundation of naturalism. By global stimulus he means the class of all sensory receptors that are triggered at a moment — the temporally ordered class of receptors triggered during the specious present.

---

[14] Zeki, 2003, "The Disunity of Consciousness".

Each global stimulus is an ordered subject of the subject's nerve-endings. Two global stimuli are said to be receptually similar if they comprise more or less the same nerve-endings in more or less the same order.

Receptual similarity is distinguished by Quine from perceptual similarity. Perceptual similarity is the effect on the subject. Two receptually very similar global stimuli are indeed apt to be perceptually similar, but two receptually very dissimilar ones can be perceptually similar too.

Another factor responsible for perceptual similarity is *salience*. Most of the receptors triggered on any occasion are not perceptually effective. Only the salient ones determine perceptual similarity among global stimuli. Quine says that the salient part is the part by virtue of which a global stimulus is perceptually similar to other global stimuli despite divergence of other parts.

Salience is, says Quine, the operative factor in ostensive definition. Sweeping or pointing gestures in the vicinity or direction of the intended portion of the scene implement the desired association with the spoken word.

Quine observes that perceptual similarity is the basis of all learning. It operates through our propensity to expect perceptually similar situations to have sequels perceptually similar to each other. Since learning hinges on perceptual similarity, perceptual similarity is not itself learned. It is innate. It can also be moulded by experience. Natural selection has endowed us with standard of perceptual similarity. Perceptual similarity of global stimuli of an individual is, in part innate and in part moulded by experience, private, but there is a public harmony of private standards of perceptual similarity. If two scenes trigger perceptually similar global stimuli in one individual they are apt to do so in another.

Learning of language, according to Quine, is based on public harmony of private standards of perceptual similarity and it is made possible by natural selection. Observation sentences constitute the building-blocks of human languages. Examples are "It is raining", It's cold", "Dog!". They report intersubjectively observable situations, observable outright. Within the individual the observation sentence is keyed to a range of perceptually fairly similar global stimuli. They qualify as observation sentences across the community. Observation sentences are the inception of language.

It seems from the kind of naturalism advocated by Quine that words are tied down to the effects in an individual of global stimuli. So sentences are tied down to the relationships between the effects of global stimuli. If such a relationship between effects of global stimuli constitutes the content of a sentence, how is it possible for a sentence to be in touch with the world at all? How is it possible for our language to represent the world at all?

This "How question" cannot be answered by giving a description of the reality. It is not a descriptive question at all. Rather it is a question of a familiar philosophical kind.

John McDowell[15] raises a similar question in the context of the relation between mind and world. He argues that talk of impressions, impingements by the world on a possessor of sensory capacities, is an empirical description. The idea of receiving an impression is the idea of a transaction in nature. Such a description cannot give an answer to the philosophical question "How can our thinking be directed to the world?" An answer to this question can be given in terms of placing certain things in the logical space of reason, which is contrasted with the logical space of nature.

Quine's naturalism, as an account of the intersubjectivity of linguistic representation, may be admitted, but it is not clear about the way in which it addresses the "How possible?" philosophical question. Since observation sentences are the inception of language, Quine's success in addressing the question in general depends upon his success in addressing the issue in particular for observation sentences. Observation sentences are learned by an individual through keying them to perceptually similar global stimuli. The public character of our observation sentences is ensured by pre-established harmony.

---

[15] McDowell, 1994, *Mind and World.*

What do these observation sentences represent? Do they represent global stimuli? If yes, then Quine's naturalism can be considered as an adequate account of linguistic representation. The Wittgensteinian charge of impossibility of private language may be avoided in terms of naturalistic idea of pre-established harmony.

The further question that Quine has to answer is: "Are truth-matters of observation sentences confined to global stimuli?" The issue of truth is closely related with the issue of linguistic representation. If a sentence represents something then the obtaining of that thing makes the sentence true. Thus if an observation sentence represents certain perceptually similar global stimuli, then it is true, if and only if such a stimulus occurs. This form of naturalism does not seem to be very different from Carnapian phenomenalism from which Quine explicitly distinguishes his naturalism.

The "How possible?" philosophical question comes in with all of its force as soon as it is admitted that truth-matters of observation sentences are outside our global stimuli. Quine seems to hold that truth-matters of observation sentences are external to our global stimuli. He says that all members of the language community are disposed to agree on the truth or falsity of such a sentence on the spot, if they have normal perception and witness to the occasions.[16] What constitutes the spot, the occasion? If it is considered to be the external situation the obtaining of which makes the observation sentence true then it becomes difficult to give an account of how the observation sentence represents the external situation.

Davidson differs from Quine with respect to what constitutes the communicable content of our sentences. For Quine, it is the global stimulus that constitutes the communicable content. An observation sentence is stimulus synonymous for two users of the concerned language between whom communication in terms

[16] Quine, 1995, *From Stimulus to Science*, p. 22.

of the observation sentence takes place. They are prompted to accept or reject the sentence by the same patterns of proximal stimulation.

Davidson is an externalist. He suggests that semantic content is determined by external objects and events, salient to both speaker and interpreter. It is determined by the very objects and events the speaker's words are taken by the interpreter to have as the subject matter. Davidson says, "It is the distal stimulus that matters to interpretation".[17] Davidson's distal theory of reference and meaning can, unlike Quine's proximal theory of reference and meaning, avoid the philosophical "How possible?" puzzle of linguistic representation. No such issue arises in the Davidsonian framework as meaning of a sentence in this framework is tied down to external objects and events.

One difficulty often pointed out against the Davidsonian distal theory is that it makes error hard to explain, the crucial gap between what is believed to be true and what is true; since the distal theory bases truth on belief, the problem is crucial.

Davidson has attempted to give his solution to this problem. Davidson's distal theory of reference and meaning encounters another difficulty that I think cannot be addressed so easily. Davidson is a direct realist. He contends that the real objects and events in the external world can be represented directly by our language.

The neuro-scientific studies provide a ground to the claim that the neural system of humans puts the limit to our knowledge of the external world. Our knowledge of the external world is shaped by our neural apparatus. A brief account of how it is so is given above. The neuro-scientific account of our knowledge of the external world suggests that the neural limit to our knowledge of the external world is a human predicament. So the Davidsonian distal theory of linguistic representation has to refute the claim of human predicament pointed out by neuro-scientists in order to

---

17 Donald Davidson, 1990, "The Structure and Content of Truth", p. 321.

achieve its strength, which, I think, is not so easy a task. Quine accommodates the predicament but fails to answer the "How possible?" question; Davidson can answer the "How possible?" question but fails to accommodate the predicament. This Quine–Davidson conflict stands in the way to the progress in the area of linguistic representation in the Western philosophy of language.

12

The Folly of Trying to Tarnish the Objectivity of Truth

THE long tradition of considering the concept of truth as one of the most important subjects of philosophical discussion has been questioned by many philosophers in contemporary philosophical discourse. The reaction ranges from giving truth an improper role to abolishing it from the philosophical arena. Examining some of the reasons behind this range of reactive theses and showing the folly of trying to tarnish truth constitute the focus of this chapter.

One of the major attacks came from the American pragmatists. The attack was directed to the attempt to present epistemology as providing the final and most basic truths on which all other truths, whether of science, morality or common sense, must rest. John Dewey, for example, made a strong protest to this kind of promise made by philosophers stating that philosophers were not privy to some special or foundational species of truth without which science could not hope to advance. He not only pointed out the falsity of the claim of philosophers having privileged access to grandeur truth, he also rejected the classical concept truth itself. The classical concept of truth is of the view that truth consists in the correspondence to the intrinsic nature of reality. His onslaught on the classical concept of truth resulted in redefining the concept of truth. He declared that a belief or theory is true if and only if it promotes human affairs. According to Richard Rorty, Dewey "agreed with Nietzsche that the traditional notion of truth, as correspondence to the intrinsic nature of reality, was a remnant of the idea of submission to the will of God."[1] Such a posture,

[1] Rorty, 1996, "Something to Steer by" (review of Alan Ryan's *John Dewey and the High Tide of American Liberalism*).

according Rorty, is infantile in its submissiveness to something other than ourselves. If human beings are to achieve maturity, they need to follow Dewey in liberating themselves from this sort of religion, a religion of abasement before the divine Other. Taking a cue from Dewey's anti-authoritarianism Rorty says that a humanism that goes no further than anti-authoritarianism in the sphere of religion is still incomplete. Humanism should be extended to the sphere of everyday and scientific investigation. In such investigations we submit to the standards constituted by things themselves, the reality. Rorty suggests that full human maturity can be achieved by acknowledging authority only if the acknowledgement does not involve abasing ourselves before something non-human. The only authority that meets this requirement is that of human consensus. We are not answerable to reality or the world, we are rather answerable to our fellows. Answerability to the world is central to the discourse of objectivity. Rorty's call is to abandon the discourse of objectivity and work instead towards extending human solidarity.[2]

Why do Dewey and the others — Rorty includes in Dewey's camp, William James, Friedrich Nietzsche, Michel Foucault and himself — put forward a thesis of truth that is clearly contrary to the ordinary concept of truth?

Rorty's argument for rejecting the idea of considering truth as correspondence is based on James's principle that a difference has to make a difference to practice before it is worth discussing. Following James, Rorty says, "Pragmatists think that if something makes no difference to practice, it should make no difference to philosophy."[3] Applying this principle to truth he perhaps wants to show that the distinction between truth and falsity does not make any difference to practice. Claiming that a belief is true instead of claiming that it is false, does not make any difference to our practice, if truth is taken to have objectivity as it is the case in the correspondence theory. Pragmatists hold that we cannot

---

[2] Rorty, 1991, "Solidarity or Objectivity".

[3] Rorty, 1995, "Is Truth a Goal of Enquiry?".

be certain that even our best researched, most successful beliefs are true if truth is taken to be objective. So truth claim of a belief fails to move us any further from a point as the falsity claim of it fails to do so. So Rorty says that philosophers cannot feel it interesting to discuss about the nature or meaning of "truth".

By contrast the difference between justified and unjustified makes a difference to our practice. When a belief is claimed to be justified, the justification claim is made relative to the audiences of the time when the claim is made. At the time of making a justification claim the claim maker is aware that the considered justification may not be taken by the distant descendants and so the belief which is claimed to be justified may look as primitive to them as those of the Greeks look to us. Unlike truth claim there is no universality claim in the claim when a belief is claimed to be justified. If a belief is taken to be justified by the fellow beings of the time when the claim is made it does make a difference to our practice. A belief being accepted as justified by the fellow beings at a particular time provides confidence to go ahead at that time, whereas it's not being accepted as justified provides diffidence. So pragmatists are keen to include the concept of justification in philosophical discussion. Truth claim does not add anything to justification claim in scientific or other enquiry. So some pragmatists conclude that truth should be reduced to justification and we should give up the idea of objectivity if it is a norm, something for which to strive.

Donald Davidson here points out that we have a choice. Instead of giving up the traditional view that truth is objective, we can give up the equally traditional view (to which some pragmatic adhere) that truth is a norm, something for which to strive. He agrees with pragmatics that we cannot consistently take truth to be both objective and something to be pursued. He suggests that it is better to cleave to a view that counts truth as objective, but pointless as goal.[4]

---

[4] Rorty, 1995, op. cit.

The concept of truth thus appears to be redundant for a pragmatist. One many ask, why does our language include the word "truth" in addition to the word "justification"? Rorty replies that "truth" has a cautionary use. We say that a belief may be justified but not true. All that is intended by this is to caution us that what is taken to be a justification for a belief now may not be taken to be so by future generations. This cautionary use of "true" subdues arrogance and brings modesty in the justification claimer. This is the role which according to pragmatists can legitimately be thought of truth. From pragmatist's perspective "true" is a misnomer if truth is viewed as a relation of correspondence between a belief and the objective reality. Rorty says that truth cannot be the goal of our enquiry if it is viewed so.[5]

The similarities and differences between the positions of Rorty and Davidson concerning truth are worth mentioning. Both of them admit that (i) we will never know for certain which of the things we belief are true; and (ii) pursuit of truth is an empty enterprise. The major difference between these two positions is that Rorty denies objectivity of truth, whereas Davidson fights tooth and nail to protect it.

Rorty has given his reason, as we have seen above, from pragmatist's point of view for denying the objectivity of truth. What is Davidson's argument for admitting the objectivity of truth?

Rorty's rejection of the objectivity of truth is based on the pragmatist principle that something is worth pursuing only if it makes a difference to our practice. Davidson perhaps respects this principle. So he agrees with Rorty that the objective truth cannot be a goal of our enquiry. Where Davidson differs from Rorty is that unlike Rorty, he does not see any reason to deny the existence of something if it does not make any difference to our practice.

Another difference between pragmatists and Davidson is that

---

[5] Davidson, 2000, "Truth, Rehabilitated".

pragmatists lay it down that any philosophical exercise concerning anything is not of genuine interest if it is not relevant to practice; since truth is not relevant to scientific practice, philosophical exercise concerning the concept of truth is not of genuine interest. Davidson contends that truth is not relevant to scientific practice and so it is not a goal of scientific enquiry, even then a theory of truth is philosophically interesting.

The reason given by Davidson for thinking the concept of truth to be interesting and important is that it has connection with meaning. He observes that this connection is used by Tarski while giving his theory of truth. In a *T*-sentence of a Tarskian theory of truth for a language, the translation of a given sentence of the language is used. This translation succeeds only if it preserves the truth of the given sentence and thereby makes the *T*-sentence true and the traditional aim of translation is to preserve meaning.

Deflationists differ from Davidson at this point. Deflationism has many forms. The idea common to different brands of deflationism is that truth, though a legitimate concept, is essentially trivial and does not deserve the grand metaphysical attention it has received. Frank Ramsey, for example, says, "[T]here is really no separate problem of truth but merely a linguistic muddle".[6] He observes that "It is true that Caesar was murdered" means no more than "Caesar was murdered": in such contexts "It is true that" simply operates like double negation, a sentential connective that maps true sentences onto true, and false sentences onto false ones. On the basis of this observation Ramsey argues that in addition to emphasis and verbosity the phrase "it is true that" adds nothing to what we can say by the use of a sentence to which the phrase is prefixed. Thus Ramey is in favour of eliminating "true" from our vocabulary. Paul Horwich, another deflationist, does not speak of elimination of the concept of truth, but he holds that it is trivial.[7] He formulates a method of

[6] Ramsey, 1990, "Facts and Propositions".

[7] Horwich, 1990.

constructing a Tarskian *T*-sentence-like sentence for every sentence of a language. For example, for the sentence "Caesar was murdered" he constructs the sentences "The proposition that Caesar was murdered is true if and only if Caesar was murdered". Horwich admits that such sentences specify precisely the circumstances under which any expressible proposition is true. He maintains that the totality of such sentences, the axiomatized system of these sentences, provides an interconnected circumstance that exhausts the content of the concept of truth.

Horwich claims that Quine and Tarski endorse deflationism. Quine has repeatedly spoken of what he calls the disquotational aspect of truth, applied to sentences, not to propositions as said by Horwich. The truth predicate is disquotational in the sense that a sentence like "'snow is white' is true" is equivalent to the result of disquoting the contained sentence and dropping the truth predicate, i.e. equivalent to "Snow is white". So, Quine is more inclined towards elimination of truth predicate. Horwich's deflationism and Quine's disquotational theory have a common feature despite differences in their interpretation of the deliverances of the truth theory. It is that the truth theory exhausts the content of the concept of truth.

Davidson contends that neither Horwich's deflationism nor Quine's disquotation can give a complete account of the concept of truth.[8] Regarding Tarski's theory, Davidson is of the opinion that Tarski's truth definitions,[9] vis-à-vis deflationism and disquotation, are not trivial, and they reveal something deep about languages of any serious expressive power. The truth conditions, specified by the *T*-sentences of a Tarski type truth definition for a language, account for the meaning of the sentences of the language. Deflationists and others tend to doubt that truth conditions have anything to do with meaning. According to them, meaning has to do with how sentences are used rather than with their truth conditions.

---

[8] Donald Davidson, 2000, op. cit.

[9] Tarski, 1956, "The Concept of Truth in Formalized Languages".

Davidson here points out a confusion. It is that truth conditional and use accounts of meaning are thought to be in competition. He holds that they are not actually so. His argument goes like this.

> It is clear that someone who knows under what condition a sentence would be true understands the sentence, and if the sentence has a truth value then someone who does not know under what conditions it would be true does not understand it. This simple claim does not rule out an account of meaning which holds that sentences mean what they do because of how they are used; it may be that they are used as they are because of their truth conditions, and they have the truth conditions they do because of how they are used.[10]

Michael Dummett appreciates Davidson's point that truth condition and use need not be thought to be at loggerheads, but it depends on the concept of truth involved in the truth conditions which, he claims, can give an account of meaning of a language. The classical concept of truth captured in Tarski's theory of truth that endorses the principle of bivalence is a recognition transcendent notion of truth. Dummett argues[11] that truth conditions involving such a concept cannot meet with use and so fail to account for meaning of a language. The knowledge of truth conditions that constitutes our understanding of a sentence, says Dummett, is of course a dispositional knowledge, a capacity. It is clear that we cannot in general equate knowledge of truth conditions with a capacity simply to state those conditions, because it will generate either circularity or infinite regress. So, Dummett suggests that knowledge of truth conditions be regarded as a recognitional capacity, viz. a capacity to recognize the truth conditions. This kind of knowledge is distinguished, by Dummett from "knowing that" and "knowing how", the two types of knowledge distinguished by Gilbert Ryle.[12] Dummett calls it "knowing what". A person having knowledge of truth condition

---

10 Davidson, 2000, op. cit., p. 70.

11 Dummett, 1976, "What *is* a Theory of Meaning (II)?".

12 Ryle, 1955, *The Concept of Mind*.

of a sentence knows what constitutes that condition the obtaining of which makes the sentence true. Dummett points out that if a person possesses knowledge of truth conditions of a sentence, the person must be in a position to recognize that the truth condition of the sentence obtains as and when a truth condition of the sentence obtains.

Dummett argues that if the truth condition of a sentence is taken classically, if truth is taken to be objective, if it endorses the principle of bivalence then the meaning of a sentence constituted by such a truth condition cannot be tied down to use. This is shown by Dummett in the context of undecidable sentences. Undecidable sentences are such that we do not possess an effective procedure for determining their truth value. We know the meaning of such sentences. If our knowing the meaning of these sentences consists in knowing the classical truth conditions of them then our knowledge can never get manifested, because according to the objectivists, we cannot recognize the truth conditions of these sentences even when they obtain, so meaning understood in terms of classical truth condition is dissociated from use.

Davidson acknowledges that by registering how a language is used that we can make it our own. But he is sceptical about the thought that there is a simple, direct, non question-begging way to employ "uses" to provide a theory of meaning. It is worth quoting Davidson at length here:[13]

> At the start the learner does not register anything more than an association between object or situation and sound or gesture. The value of the association is supplied by the teacher or the environment in the form of reward. In the beginning there is not a word but a sound being given a use. The teacher sees the learner as picking up a bit of language with a meaning already there; the learner has no idea of prior meaning or use, for the learner what was meaningless before now takes on significance. In the early stage of ostensive learning, error has no point for the learner, for there is nothing for him to be wrong about, and

13 Davidson, 2000, op. cit., p. 71.

> where error has no point, there is not a concept or thought. Once trial and error (from the teacher's point of view) is replaced with thought and belief (from the learner's point of view), the concept of truth has application.

Davidson distinguishes the phase of ostensive learning from the phase of learning some grammar of a language. In the former phase a child is of more than a pragmatist. Once some grammar is in hand, separately learned parts can be assembled in new ways, and truth separates from the merely useful or approved. In this phase a learner may generate meaningful sentences, the use of which is never encountered by the learner. By the use of such sentences the learner expresses thought or certain conditions the obtaining of which makes the sentences true. It is the step from reacting to proximal stimuli to the thought of distal stimuli, the step, Davidson says, from mere conditioned response to what Wittgenstein called "following a rule". Truth comes into picture at the phase of rule following.

John McDowell, like Dummett, agrees with Davidson that the concept of truth is connected with the concept of meaning. He is more engaged in rehabilitating the objectivity of truth that Rorty tellingly deplores. He appreciates Rorty's attempt to cure ourselves of unwarranted expectations for philosophy, but he warns of dropping the vocabulary of objectivity that Rorty resorts to as a way to the cure.[14] McDowell points out that the vocabulary of objectivity out of the important tasks of philosophers is to understand the source of the deformations and undo the deformations thereafter. This would be an epistemological achievement because it would enable us to see our way clear of the seemingly compulsory philosophical problematic.

McDowell argues that Rorty's view that the only hygienically available conception of what it is for, say, a claim to be justified (or warranted or rationally acceptable) must be relative to some particular audience leads to philosophical trouble no less than the deformed objectivity of truth.

---

[14] McDowell, 2000, "Towards Rehabilitating Objectivity".

R.C. Pradhan observes that Rorty's attempt to reject the concept of truth results from his obsession, as a pragmatist, with the epistemological notion of justification.[15] He points out that the concept of justification involves the concept of truth. When we give a justification, the justification is given for establishing the truth of a sentence or of a belief. So without the concept of truth, the concept of justification cannot be grasped.

McDowell contends that we can make sense of a notion of justification for which the relevant question is "in the light of what?" but we cannot make sense of a notion of justification for which the question is "to whom?" as emphasized by Rorty.

The purported ground of Rorty's phobia around truth is that if we conceive truth as a mode of justifiedness that transcends consensus, we are conceiving something that would not be achievable. McDowell distinguishes between innocuous transcendence and illusory transcendence, and argues for innocuous transcendence. The kind of truth that innocuously transcends consensus is not an ever retreating goal. The difference between the two kinds of transcendence, illusory and innocuous, pointed out by McDowell is that in the former case we have a picture of representation which relates our thought and language to something more independent of us than the world as it figures in our world-view, whereas in the latter case we have a picture of representation which relates our thought and language to the world as it figures in our world-view. The former position is what Hilary Putnam calls "metaphysical" realism as, McDowell, following Kant, calls it "transcendental" realism.

The former view of representation leads philosophers like Davidson to hold that "we could never tell which of our beliefs are true". In the latter view of representation, that McDowell calls "transcendental idealism", any attempt to derive the Cartesian idea that "perhaps all of our beliefs about the world may be false" is prevented. The kind of objectivity of truth thought of in the

---

15 Pradhan, 2011, "Why Care for Truth?: Rorty versus Davidson".

latter view, where the world to which our thought and language relate is not out of reach as it was in the first meditation, is different from the Davidsonian kind of objectivity. McDowell makes an eloquent effort to retain the objectivity of truth and does so in a form that allows us to see it as a goal of enquiry. He wants to retain both truth's transcendence of consensus and accessibility to the world to which our thought and language relate. Putnam and Dummett in his later writings want to do the same thing in their own ways.

The key idea of the kind of objectivity McDowell endorses is conforming to the world as it figures in our world-view. Akeel Bilgrami[16] sees similarity between McDowell's version of objective truth to Quine's position regarding truth. Quine says that we judge truth from within our current ongoing theory of the world.[17] To lay claim to this idea is to say with McDowell that the expression "true" signifies a kind of conformity of our beliefs or sentences have "to things as they figure in our world-view", "and to nothing more independent to our world-view". If McDowell and Quine are right then we do not have to accept that idea of truth according to which we cannot know which of our beliefs are true, and there is a perfectly good sense that truth is a norm and a goal of inquiry.

A Davidsonian would reject McDowell's view of truth on the ground that it fails to retain the full prestige of "truth". It might be argued that all that such a view can show is that our judgements of truth are made or that our justification of beliefs or sentences are given in the light of our best evolving doctrine. But that is not much more than trivial. So McDowell fails to provide, although promises to do so an alternative conception of objective truth.

For Davidson truth is external, the world our thought and language relate to is independent of us; our beliefs and sentences are made true by the independent world. Our beliefs are answerable to the independent world.

---

16 Akeel Bilgrami, 2000, "Is Truth a Goal of Inquiry?: Rorty and Davidson on Truth".

17 Quine, 1964, *Word and Object*.

The concept of objective truth, according to Davidson, makes our understanding of sentences possible. He says:

> Given degrees of belief and the relative strengths of desire for the truth of interpreted sentences, we can give a propositional content to the beliefs and desires of an agent.[18]

So one can say the concept of truth is essential to understanding others and explaining why they act as they do. The various propositional attitudes sentences are used to express also depend on the concept of objective truth. I quote Davidson here:

> I can believe it is now raining, but this is because I know that whether or not it is raining does not depend on whether I believe it, or everyone believes it, or it is useful to believe it, it is up to nature, not to me or my society or the entire history of human race. . . . Without a grasp of the concept of truth not only language but thought itself, is impossible.[19]

Davidson repeatedly makes it clear that although he admits the objectivity of truth, he does not endorse the view that truth is radically non-epistemic, that all of our best researched and established beliefs and theories may be false. He recognizes that truth must somehow be related to the attitudes of rational creatures. In this respect Davidson has agreement with the pragmatists, but he rejects pragmatism and all epistemic theories of truth on the ground that they reduce reality to much less than we believe there is.

Rorty's suggestion to abolish the objectivity of truth on the ground that it is an ever-retreating goal in our inquiry is not endorsed by Davidson, because he is convinced that speakers in a language largely share views and what they share is a largely correct picture of a common world. But if the world is independent of us how is it possible to have access to truth of our sentences or beliefs about the world? Davidson's reply is that the normativity of the thought, desire and action of the speaker and the interpreter

---

18 Davidson, 2000, op. cit., p. 72.

19 Donald Davidson, 2005, *Truth and Predication.*

who are rational beings makes our access to the objectivity of truth and communication possible. Davidson says:

> The ultimate source of both objectivity and communication is the triangle that, by relating speaker, interpreter and the world, determines the contents of thought and speech. Given this source, there is no room for a relativized concept of truth.[20]

Davidson and McDowell agree on the point that transcendental realism is unacceptable. They also try to rehabilitate the objectivity of truth against the attempt to abolish it by pragmatists like Rorty. McDowell tries to do so by claiming that the world our sentences and beliefs relate to is the world that figures in our world-view. Davidson is against this kind of transcendental idealism on the ground that it does not give full prestige to truth. For Davidson the world to which our sentences and beliefs relate is completely independent of us, but the truth that emerges from the relation between our sentences and belief on one hand and the world on the other is made accessible to us by the normativity of our thought, desire and action originating from the rationality of the speaker and the interpreter. Thus Davidson shows that the pragmatists like Rorty have a phobia in their attempt to abolish the objectivity of truth. Their fear is completely irrational.

Michael Dummett's worry about giving an account of understanding of undecidable sentences from the perspective of Davidsonian truth condition theory of meaning is also not rationally grounded. Knowledge of truth of the beliefs associated with the *T*-sentences corresponding to the undecidable sentences is attained through their coherence with the set of beliefs associated with the *T*-sentences corresponding to other sentences. I have discussed this in detail in chapter 9.

---

[20] See Chakraborti, 2000, *Realism and Its Alternatives.*

13

On Empathic Reasoning

> We need not just logic but EMPATHY. The capacity for logical thought is one of the things that makes us human. What distinguishes those who thrive is their ability to understand what makes their fellow women or men tick, to forge relationships, and care for others.
>
> — Daniel H. Pink, 2000, *A Whole New Mind*, p. 66

"EMPATHY" is widely used in psychotherapy, medical science and ethics, and recently in Artifical Intelligence (AI) and cognitive science. Here I shall discuss about the structure of empathy involved in psychotherapy.

In answer to the question "What is empathy?" people often say that empathy is "Putting oneself in the shoes of others" or "Getting under the skin of others". These metaphorical definitions of the word "empathy" do give an idea of what empathy is, but the nuances involved in empathy need elaboration in order to have a clear perception of the structure of empathy.

How do we know other minds? There is a prolonged debate in philosophy over this issue. Philosophers often go further and ask whether we can know other minds at all. In psychotherapy knowledge of other minds is taken for granted. So they give answer to the above question and their answer is that we know other minds by means of empathy. Thus in psychotherapy empathy is viewed as a process by which we know truths about another person's mental world.

Since empathy is regarded as a canon of knowledge, researchers are engaged in formulating the structure of empathy — the process by which we know facts of the mental worlds of others. This logical issue has been seriously addressed, among others, by Alvin Goldman, Allison Barnes and Paul Thagard. They hold that empathy is a form of analogical thinking.

Goldman's account of empathy is called the simulation theory.[1] He says that to empathize a person is to ascribe to that person mental states which are simulated in us. He explains the process in the following way.

We feign the beliefs and desires of another person, feed these inputs into our own practical reasoning mechanisms; the output states which we generate are subsequently taken "off-line" and attributed to that person.

So, according to Goldman, mental states of others are inferred by analogy of our own mental states. Goldman's theory intends to deflate the well-established position in the debate on the nature of mental state ascription, known as "theory theory", which states that understanding minds of others is a matter of applying some theory of mind to them.

A theory theorist would say, for example, that we ascribe the belief "I am inadequate" to a person who fumbles while presenting something to a group of significant seniors. The ascription of this belief to the person is based on the application to the person of the theory — If a person believes that s/he is inadequate in presenting something before a group of people then s/he feels anxious in presenting the thing to the group and as a result s/he fumbles. Thus according to a theory theorist, empathy is a rule-based reasoning, where rules are constituted by the principles of mind of if . . . then . . . form.

A simulation theorist like Goldman espouses as an alternative to the theory theory that we habitually understand beliefs, desires, etc. of another person, in the absence of any theory of mind, by using the resources of our own mind; we can simulate beliefs and intentions of others in our own mind based on some behavioural

---

1 Goldman, 1993, *Philosophical Applications of Cognitive Science;* 1992, "In Defence of the Simulation Theory".

cues, and consequently ascribe these beliefs and intentions to that person.

Barnes and Thagard[2] contend that empathy is best viewed as a kind of analogical thinking, but their account of empathy is different from that of Goldman. Goldman's simulation theory and the theory theory are competing theories of empathy; but Barnes–Thagard theory of empathy shows that the assumption that the theory theory and the simulation theory are mutually exclusive alternatives is a false assumption. They hold that empathy always involves simulation, but may simultaneously include theory application. Empathy is independent of theory application when an analog of another's mental state is easily retrieved from memory. Processes of rule-based reasoning are required when empathy is achieved by constructing an analog. The constraints of analogical mapping determine when an analog is likely to be retrieved and when it is likely to be constructed.

Barnes and Thagard consider analogy as a computational process of finding correspondences between complex structures that involve relations between objects and causal relations between relations. Analogy involves a system mapping between a source analog and a target analog. Target analog is the system to be understood, and source analog is the system from which the analogical inference is made.

Let us consider a case of empathic reasoning involving only simulation, and no theory application.

The following is the system mapping between a person's having been fired from a valued job and Hamlet's distress when his uncle killed his father and married his mother.

Source: You	*Target: Hamlet*
Fire (boss, you): *s*1 — fire	Kill (uncle, father): *t*1 — kill
Lose (you, job): *s*2 — lose	Lose (Hamlet, father): *t*2 — lose
	Marry (uncle, mother): *t*3 — marry

[2] Barnes and Thagard, 1997, "*Empathy and Analogy*".

Cause (*s1* — fire, *s2* — lose): *s3*	Cause (*t1* — kill, *t2* — lose): *t3a*
Angry (you): *s4* — angry	Angry (Hamlet): *t4* — angry
Depressed (you): *s5* — depressed	Depressed (Hamlet): *t5* — depressed
Cause (*s2* — lose, *s4* — angry): *s6*	Cause (*t2* — lose, *t4* — angry): *t6*
Cause (*s2* — lose, *s5* — depressed): *s7*	Cause (*t2* — lose, *t5* — depressed): *t7*
Indecisive (you): *s8* — indecisive	
Cause (*s5* — depressed, *s8* — indecisive): *s9*	

On the basis of the correspondences from *s1*-*t1* to *s7*-*t7* and *s9* you can infer *t8*: indecisive (Hamlet).

This last inference involves a process that Keith Holyoak and Thagard[3] call "copying-with-substitution:" to expand the Hamlet target, you copy over from the source the predicate indecisive, and substitute Hamlet for you on the basis of the mapping already established.

On the Barnes–Thagard theory of analogy mapping between source and target does not require semantic identity of relations such as fire and kill, or exact structural correspondence between source and target, e.g. the boss fired you does not exactly match with the uncle killed the father, not Hamlet.

Barnes and Thagard argue that the simulation theory cannot account for our empathic understanding of someone of a different culture, or someone who is mentally impaired, because the other person is very different from us, it may be very difficult for us to find a source analog from our own experience that has features and causal structures that are similar to the other person. Donna Williams[4] describes how her autistic traits were almost always misunderstood. Barnes and Thagard would say that this misunderstanding was due to attempts to understand Donna's affective state in the simulation theory model.

According to them, a correct empathic understanding of Donna's affective states requires a background theory in the form of rule-based reasoning, specifically about the nature of autism.

[3] Holyoak and Thagard, 1995, *Mental Leaps*.

[4] Williams, 1992, *Nobody Nowhere*.

So a non-autistic has to construct a source analog or affective schema that includes, at minimum, feelings of intense isolation and frustration. This constructed analog will make simulation possible. Then by "copying-with substitution" s/he can infer Donna's affective states. Empathy is particularly likely to fail if we are not motivated to go to the effort of constructing an appropriate source analog when no such analog can be retrieved.

The account of empathy given in Barnes–Thagard theory has the following important implication:

> The assumption that the theory-theory (understanding other people is a matter of applying some "theory of mind" to them) and the simulation theory (we understand others' mental states by simulating them in our minds) are mutually exclusive alternatives is a false assumption. Empathy always involves simulation but may simultaneously include theory application.

But neither Goldman's simulation theory nor Barmes–Thagard theory is a satisfactory account of empathy.

Argument 1

Both the simulation theory and Barnaes–Thagard theory view empathy as a form of analogical thinking, and so both of them admit simulation of mental states or construction of mental states by analogy with which we understand others' mental states.

But this goes against what Carl Rogers,[5] the pioneer of humanistic psychotherapy in which the concept of empathy occupies the central place, says in explaining what empathy is.

Rogers says:

> Empathic understanding is perceiving the hates and hopes and fears of the client through immersion in an empathic process, but without himself, as a counselor, experiencing these hates and hopes and fears.

As simulation consists in experiencing these mental facts

[5] Carl R. Rogers, 1951, *Client-centered Therapy*.

Goldman's simulation theory and the Barnes–Thagard theory cannot capture what empathy actually is. What these theories capture is close to sympathy rather than to empathy. Lauren Wispe[6] describes the difference between sympathy and empathy in the following way:

1. In empathy the self is the vehicle for understanding, and it never loses its identity; sympathy is concerned with communion.
2. In empathy one substitutes oneself for the other person; in sympathy one substitutes others for oneself.
3. Empathy is a way of knowing; sympathy is a way of relating.

The concept of copying with substitution involved in analogical account of empathy clearly shows that Goldman's theory and Barnes–Thagard theory characterize sympathy, not empathy.

Argument 2

Rogers says:

> In empathic understanding the counsellor assumes the internal frame of reference of the client: the counsellor perceives the world as the client sees it, the counsellor perceives the client himself as he is seen by himself. The counsellor has to lay aside all perceptions from the external frame of reference (the counsellor's frame of reference) while understanding someone empathically.

But in Goldman's simulation theory as well as in Barnesy–Thagard theory one cannot lay aside one's frame of reference. So neither of these two theories can give a satisfactory account of empathy.

I agree with Goldman and Barnes–Thagard that the empathic process involved in empathic understanding is a form of inference. But I differ from them in saying that it is a form of analogical thinking.

One might say that empathy is a form of perception. We can see different mental states of a person on the face of the person.

---

[6] Wispe, 1991, *The Psychology of Empathy*.

I do not agree that what we see on the face of a person are mental states of the person, they are rather facial expressions of mental states of the person. Paul Ekman and W.V. Friesen[7] have conducted cross-cultural studies to show that facial expressions of the same mental state might vary in different cultures.

I think that empathic reasoning is a form of abduction. Charles Sanders Peirce[8] coined the term "abduction" to describe that initial phase in scientific discovery when a bold hypothesis is formed to explain some surprising fact or observation. It is a creative process.

Peirce regarded Kepler's discovery of the elliptical orbit of Mars to be a classic example of abduction. Kepler's reasoning was as follows:

First, the surprising fact of certain irregularities in the path of Mars is observed. But if the orbit of Mars were elliptical, then these movements would be a matter of course. So hypothetically, Mars travels in an elliptical orbit. Thus an abductive reasoning runs like this. *A* surprising fact, *C* is observed, But, if *A* were true, then, *C* would be matter of course. So, hypothetically, *A*.

Schematically,

C

If *A* then *C*.

So, *A*.

Of course, this hypothesis can only be entertained tentatively, awaiting testing by further observation and reasoning. This phase in scientific enquiry is where the creative element enters. It has been described as conjecture — the result of intuition, a leap of the imagination or a guess, although not mere guess. The hypothesis reached through abduction is a bold hypothesis. Abduction contrasts with the process of reasoning (deduction or induction) by which we test or justify our hypothesis. The conjectural knowledge of this kind constitutes an epistemological

---

[7] Ekman and Friesen, 1975, *Unmasking the Face*.

[8] Peirce, 1966, "Abduction, Induction and Deduction" .

paradigm, which is different from but complementary to the paradigm of scientific knowledge (i.e. deduction and induction).

Abduction is different from deduction. In a deductive argument the premises imply the conclusion. It is the application of a rule to a particular case, e.g.

If *A* then *C*

A

So, *C*.

By contrast, abduction is not the application of a rule to a case. If it were it would be fallacious — the fallacy of affirming the consequent. Unlike the case of valid deduction true premises in an abduction do not guarantee the truth of the conclusion, abduction involves presumption to truth. The conclusion of an abductive inference is held interrogatively, as a question. We cannot affirm its conclusion with certitude. It involves an amount of risk. However, correlated with this element of risk is an element of inventiveness or originality. It creates new knowledge. This distinguishes it from induction.

By the use of empathy, in an abductive reasoning we understand the facts of the mental world of the client — the beliefs, desires, hopes and feelings and their interrelations. Associations of ideas provide the basis of empathy. On the basis of empathy we build up a coherent picture or explanation of the client's symptoms.

Empathy as an abductive reasoning does provide us with an understanding of the mental world of the client. But understanding of another's mind is not all of empathy. In psychotherapy empathy has got three aspects — empathic understanding, empathic resonance and empathic communication. So far I have discussed only empathic understanding — how understanding of other minds is generated through empathy.

Empathic resonance is the resonance of the feeling the client experiences. When an understanding of the mental world of the client is generated in the system of the psychotherapist the psychotherapist feels like the client. This feeling is not the kind of feeling present in sympathy. Unlike the feeling in sympathy the feeling in empathy is a result of understanding the client's mental world when the psychotherapist assumes the client's frame of reference. The empathic resonance is the wave of feeling that reaches the psychotherapist's mind from the mind of the client through the psychotherapist's empathic understanding.

Empathic communication is the expression of this empathic resonance. This expression may be verbal or non-verbal. Through this expression the client understands that s/he is understood by the psychotherapist. This understanding of the client is extremely important in psychotherapy, because the progress of the therapy depends mostly on it.

Bibliography

Anderson, J.R., 1983, *The Architecture of Cognition*, Cambridge, MA: Harvard University Press.

Ayer, A.J., 1956, *The Problem of Knowledge*, London: Penguin Books.

———, 1958, *The Foundations of Empirical Knowledge*, London: Macmillan.

———, 1969, *Philosophical Essays*, London: Macmillan.

———, 1973, *The Central Questions of Philosophy*, London: Penguin.

Banerjee, K.K., 1979, "The Doctrine of Triple Negation in Neo-Nyaya Logic", *Jadavpur Studies in Philosophy*, vol. I.

Barnes, Allison and Paul Thagard, 1997, "Empathy and Analogy", in *Dialogue: Canadian Philosophical Review*.

Banerjee, Hiranmoy, 1997, "Bhartrihari: A Modern Perspective", in *Essays in Indian Philosophy: Jadavpur Studies in Philosophy*, ed. Sukharanjan Saha, New Delhi: Allied Publishers.

Belnap, N., 1962, "Tonk, Plonk and Plink", *Analysis*, 22(6):130-34.

Bhattacharyya, Sibajiban, 1997, "Introduction to the Navya-Nyāya Theory of Language", in *Essays in Indian Philosophy*, ed. Sukharanjan Saha, Kolkata: Allied Publishers in collaboration with Department of Philosophy, Jadavpur University.

Bilgrami, Akeel, 1986, "Meaning, Holism and Use" in *Truth and Interpretation*, ed. Ernst Lepore, New York: Blackwell.

———, 2000, "Is Truth a Goal of Inquiry?: Rorty and Davidson on Truth", in *Rorty and His Critics*, ed. Robert B. Brandom, Oxford: Blackwell.

Brandom, Robert B., 2000, *Articulating Reasons: An Introduction to Inferentialism*, Cambridge, MA: Harvard University Press.

———, 2007, "Inferentialism and Some of Its Challenges", in *Philosophy and Phenomenological Research*, 74: 651-76.

Brentano, F., 1995, *Psychology from an Empirical Standpoint*, tr. C. Rancurello Antos, D.B. Terre and Linda L. McAlister, London: Routledge.

Buck, Ross and C. Arthur VanLear, 2002, "Verbal and Non-verbal Communication: Distinguishing Symbolic, Spontaneous, and Pseudo-Spontaneous Nonverbal Behaviour", *Journal of Communication*, Special Issue.

Chakraborti, Somnath, 1998, "Tractatus-e-Maulobakya Prasanga' ["Tractatus on Elementary Propositions"] in *Wittgensteiner Darshan*, ed. Prahlad Kumar Sarkar and Somnath Chakraborti, Darshan O Samaj Trust.

Chakraborti, Sadhan, 1998, "Semantic Holism verus Intentional Realism: An Informational Semanticist's Approach", *Journal of Indian Council of Philosophical Research*, XVI(1).

Chakraborti, Sadhan, 2000, *Realism and Its Alternatives: Some Contemporary Issues*, Kolkata: Papyrus.

Chomsky, Noam, 1964, "A Review of Skinner B.F.'s Verbal Behaviour", in *The Structure of Language*, ed. J.A. Fodor and J.J. Katz, Englewood Cliffs, NJ: Prentice-Hall.

———, 1980, *Rules and Representations*, Oxford: Blackwell.

Dasgupta, Amitabha, 1992, "Wittgenstein on Mathematical Necessity", *Journal of Indian Council of Philosophical Research*, IX(3).

Davidson, Donald, 1984, *Inquiries into Truth and Interpretation*, Oxford: Clarendon Press.

———, 1986a, "A Coherence Theory of Truth and Knowledge", in *Truth and Interpretation: Perspectives on the Philosophy of Donald Davidson*, Oxford: Basil Blackwell.

———, 1986b, "Empirical Content", in *Truth and Interpretation*, ed. Ernest Lepore, New York: Blackwell.

———, 1986c, "A Nice Derangement of Epitaphs", in *Truth and Interpretation: Perspectives on the Philosophy of Donald Davidson*, ed. Ernest Lepore, Oxford: Basil Blackwell.

———, 1990, "The Structure and Content of Truth", *The Journal of Philosophy*, 87(6).

———, 2000, "Truth, Rehabilitated", in *Rorty and His Critics*, ed. Robert B. Brandom, Oxford: Blackwell.

———, 2005, *Truth and Predication*, Cambridge, MA: Belknap Press.

Devitt, M., 1991, "The Methodology of Naturalistic Semantics", *Journal of Philosophy*, 91: 545-72.

Diamond, C., 1991, *Realism and the Realistic Spirit: Wittgenstein, Philosophy and the Mind*, Cambridge, MA: MIT Press.

——— (ed.), 1993, *Wittgenstein's Lectures on the Foundations of Mathematics*, Cambridge: Cornell University Press, first published in Ithaca, 1976.

Dretske, F., 1981, *Knowledge and the Flow of Information*, Cambridge, MA: MIT Press.

Dummett, Michael, 1973, *Frege: Philosophy of Language*, London: Duckworth.

———, 1976, "What Is a Theory of Meaning II?", in *Truth and Meaning*, ed. G. Evans and J. McDowell, Oxford: Clarendon Press.

———, 1977, *Elements of Intuitionism*, Oxford: Clarendon Press.

———, 1978a, "The Justification of Deduction", in *Truth and Other Enigmas*, London: Duckworth.

———, 1978b, "Truth", in *Truth and Other Enigmas*, London: Duckworth.

———, 1978c, "Wittgenstein's Philosophy of Mathematics", in *Truth and Other Enigmas*, London: Duckworth.

———, 1981, "Realism", *The Interpretation of Frege's Philosophy*, London: Duckworth.

———, 1982, "Realism", *Synthese*, 52(1): 55-112.

———, 1984, "What is a Theory of Meaning? (II)", in *Truth and Meaning*, ed. Gareth Evans and McDwell, Oxford: Clarendon Press.

———, 1989, "Language and Communication", in *Reflections on Chomsky*, ed. Alexander George, Oxford: Basil Blackwell.

———, 1991, *The Logical Basis of Metaphysics*, Cambridge, MA: Harvard University Press.

Ekman, Paul, 1980, "Biological and Cultural Contribution to Body and Facial Movement in the Expression of Emotion", in *Explaining Emotions*, ed. Amelie Oksenberg Rorty, Oakland, CA: University of California Press.

Ekman, Paul and W.V. Friesen, 1975, *Unmasking the Face: A Guide to Recognizing Emotions from Facial Cues*, New Jersey: Prentice Hall.

Etchemendy, J., 1990, *The Concept of Logical Consequence*, Cambridge, MA: Harvard University Press.

Evans, G. and J. McDowell (eds.), 1976, *Truth and Meaning*, Oxford: Clarendon Press.

Feldman, J.A., 1985, "Connectionist Models and their Applications: Introduction", *Cognitive Science*, vol. 9.

Fillmore, C.J., 1981, "Pragmatics and the Description of Discourse", in *Radical Pragmatics*, ed. P. Cole, New York: Academic Press.

Fodor, Jerry A., 1981, *Representations*, Cambridge, Mass.: MIT Press.

———, 1988, *Psychosemantics: The Problem of Meaning in the Philosophy of Mind*, Cambridge, Massachusetts: MIT Press.

———, 1998, *Concepts*, Oxford: Clarendon Press.

Fodor, Jerry A. and E. Lepore, 1993, *Holism: A Shopper's Guide*, Cambridge, Massachusetts: MIT Press.

Frege, Gottlob, 1953, *The Foundations of Arithmetic*, tr. J.L. Austin, Oxford: Basil Blackwell.

———, 1964, *The Basic Laws of Arithmetic*, tr. and ed. M. Furth, Berkeley and Los Angeles: The University of California Press.

Gazzaniga, Michael S., Richard B. Ivry and George Mangun, 2002, *Cognitive Neuroscience: The Biology of the Mind*, 2nd edn. New York: Norton.

Gerrard, Steve, 1996, "A Philosophy of Mathematics Between Two Camps", in *The Cambridge Companion to Wittgenstein*, ed. Hans Sluga and David G.

Stern, Cambridge: Cambridge University Press.

Goldie, Peter, 2002, *Understanding Emotions: Minds and Morals*, Burlington ,VT/ Sydney: Ashgate.

Goldman, Alvin, 1992, "In Defense of the Simulation Theory", *Mind and Language*, 7(1-2): 104-19.

———, 1993, *Philosophical Applications of Cognitive Science*, Boulder, CO: Westview Press.

Goodman, N., 1977, *The Structure of Appearance*, Holland/Boston: Springer.

Grice, Paul, 1968, "Utterer's Meaning, Sentence Meaning, and Word Meaning", *Foundations of Language*, 4: 225-42.

———, 1975a, "Logic and Conversation", *Syntax and Semantics*, ed. P. Cole and Morgan, vol. 3: *Speech Acts*, New York: Academic Press.

———, 1975b, "Method in Philosophical Psychology: From Banal to the Bizarre", Proceedings and Addresses of the American Philosophical Association.

———, 1989, *Studies in the Way of Words*, Cambridge, CA: Harvard University Press.

Hans-Johann, Glock, 1996, "Necessity and Normativity", in *The Cambridge Companion to Wittgenstein*, ed. Hans Sluga and David G. Stem, Cambridge: Cambridge University Press.

Hardy, G.H., 1967, *A Mathematician's Apology*, Cambridge: Cambridge University Press.

Heyting, A., 1971, *Intuitionism*, Amsterdam: North-Holland Publishing Co.

Holyoak, Keith J. and Paul Thagard, 1995, *Mental Leaps*, Cambridge, MA: MIT Press.

Horwich, Paul, 1990, *Truth*, Oxford: Blackwell.

Hume, David, 1967, *An Enquiry Concerning Human Understanding*, Calcutta: Progressive Publishers.

James, William, 1890, *Principles of Psychology*, 2 vols., New York: Holt.

Kaplan, D., 1978, "D that" *Syntax and Semantics*, vol. 9.

———, 1989, "Afterthoughts' and 'Demonstratives", in *Themes from Kaplan*, ed. J. Almog, H. Wettstein and J. Perry, New York: Oxford University Press.

———, 1990, "Words", *Aristotelian Society Proceedings*, Supplementary vol. 64.

Kosslyn, S.M., 1983, *Ghosts in the Mind's Machine: Creating and Using Images in the Brain*, New York: Norton.

Kripke, Saul A., 1965, "Semantical Analysis of Intuitionistic Logic I", in *Formal Systems and Recursive Functions*, ed. J.N. Crossley and M.A.E. Dummett, Amsterdam: North Holland Publishing Company.

Laird, J.E. and P.S. Rosenbloom, 1987, "Soar: An Architecture for General Intelligence", *Artificial Intelligence* 33(1).

Levinson, S.C., 1983, *Pragmatics*, London: Cambridge University Press.

Lovibond, Sabina, 1983, *Realism and Imagination in Ethics*, Oxford: Blackwell.

McDowell, J., 1994, *Mind and World*, Cambridge, MA: Harvard University Press.

———, 2000, "Towards Rehabilitating Objectivity", in *Rorty and His Critics*, ed. Robert B. Brandom, Oxford: Blackwell.

Montague, R., 1970, "Universal Grammar", in *Theoria*, vol. 36.

Mukhopadhyay, Ranjan, 2000, "Individual Deduction, Rule of Inference and Validity", in *Realism, Responses and Reactions: Essays in Honour of Pranab Kumar Sen*, ed. D.P. Chattopadhyay, Sandhya Basu, Madhabendra Nath Mitra and Ranjan Mukhopadhyay, New Delhi: Indian Council of Philosophical Research.

Neale, Stephen, 1992, "Paul Grice and the Philosophy of Language", *Linguistics and Philosophy*, 15(5).

Newell, Allen and H.A. Simon, 1963, "Computers in Psychology", in *Handbook of Mathematical Psychology*, vol. I, ed. R.D. Luce, R.R. Bush and E. Galantet, New York/London: John Wiley.

Newell, Allen, Paul S. Rosenbloom and John E. Laird, 1996, "Symbolic Architectures for cognition", in *Foundations of Cognitive Science*, ed. Michael I. Posner, Cambridge, MA: The MIT Press.

Quine, W.V., 1969, *Ontological Relativity and Other Essays*, New York / London: Columbia University Press.

Peirce, C.S., 1966, "Abduction, Induction and Deduction", in *Collected Papers of Charles Sanders Peirce*, ed. A.W. Burks, vol. VII, Cambridge, MA: Belknap Press.

Pradhan, Ramesh Chandra, 2011, "Why Care for Truth? Rorty versus Davidson", *Indian Journal of Analytic Philosophy*, 5(1).

Prawitz, Dag, 1987, "Dummett on a Theory of Meaning", in *Michael Dummett*, ed. Barry M. Taylor, Dordrecht: Martinus Nijhoff.

Prior, Arthur, 1960, "The Runabout Inference-Ticket", *Analysis*, 21(2): 38-39.

Putnam, Hilary, 1988, *Many Faces of Realism*, Chichago, IL: Open Court.

———, 1994, "Sense, Non-sense, and the Senses: An Enquiry into the Powers of the Human Mind", *The Journal of Philosophy*, 91(9).

———, 1997, "Putnam's Dewey Lectures", *Theoria Revista de Teoría, Historia y Fundamentos de la Ciencia*, 12(2).

Pylyshyn, Zenon W., "Computing in Cognitive Science", in *Foundations of Cognitive Science*, ed. Micheal I. Posner, Cambridge, MA: The MIT Press.

Quine, W.V, 1964, *Word and Object*, Cambridge, MA: MIT Press.

———, 1995, *From Stimulus to Science*, Cambridge, MA: Harvard University Press.

Quinton, A., 1973, *The Nature of Things*, London: Routledge and Kegan Paul.

Ramsey, Frank Plumpton, 1990, "Facts and Propositions", in *Philosophical Papers,* ed. D.H. Mellor, Cambridge: Cambridge University Press.

Recananti, Francois, 1993, *Direct Reference: From Language to Thought,* Oxford: Blackwell.

Rich, E., 1983, *Artificial Intelligence,* New York: McGraw-Hill.

Rogers, Carl R., 1951, *Client-centered Therapy: Its Current Practice, Implications and Theory,* Boston: Houghton Mifflin.

Rorty, Richard, 1991, "Solidarity or Objectivity", in *Rorty's Objectivity, Relativism and Truth,* Cambridge: Cambridge University Press.

———, 1995, "Is Truth a Goal of Enquiry: "Davidson vs. Wright", *Philosophical Quarterly,* 45(180): 281-300.

———, 1996, "Something to Steer by (review of Alan Ryan's *John Dewey and the High Tide of American Liberalism)", London Review of Books,* 18(12).

Rumelhart, D.E., 1997, "The Architecture of Mind: A Connectionist Approach" *Mind Design II,* ed. John Haugeland, Cambridge, MA: The MIT Press.

Russell, Bertrand, 1959, *The Problems of Philosophy,* Oxford: Oxford University Press.

Ryle, Gilbert, 1955, *The Concept of Mind,* London: Hutchinson's University Library.

Sartre, J.P., 1962, *Imagination: A Psychological Critique,* tr. F. Williams, Paris: University of Michigan Press.

Searle, J.R., 1975, "A Taxonomy of Illocutionary Acts", in *Language, Mind and Knowledge,* ed. K. Gunderson, Minnesota Studies in the Philosophy of Science, vol. II, Minneapolis: University of Minnesota Press.

———, 1980, "Minds, Brains and Programs", *Behavioural and Brain Sciences,* 3: 417-24.

Searle, John, 1988, "Minds and Brains without Programs". in *Mindwaves,* ed. Blackmore and Greenfield, Oxford: Basil Blackwell.

Sen, Pranab Kumar, 1991a, "On the Problem of Justifying Deduction", in *Reference and Truth,* New Delhi: Indian Council of Philosophical Research and Allied Publishers.

———, 1991b, *Reference and Truth,* New Delhi: Indian Council of Philosophical Research and Allied Publishers.

Shaw, J.L., 1985, "Proper Names: Contemporary Philosophy and the Nyāya", in *Analytical Philosophy in Comparative Perspective,* ed. J.L. Shaw and B.K. Matilal, Holland: D. Reidel.

Shaw, J.L., 2000, "Conditions for Understanding the Meaning of a Sentence: The Nyaya and the Advaita Vedanta", *Journal of Indian Philosophy,* vol. 28.

Simon, Herbert A. and Criag A. Kaplan, 1996, "Foundations of Cognitive Science", in *Foundations of Cognigtive Science,* ed. Michael I. Posner, Cambridge, MA: The MIT Press.

Strawson, P.F., 1950, "On Referring", *Mind*, vol. 59.

———, 1952, *Introduction to Logical Theory*, London: Methuen.

Tarski, Alfred, 1956, "The Concept of Truth in Formalised Languages", in *Logic, Semantics and Metamathematics*, tr. J.H. Woodger, Oxford: Oxford University Press.

Tennant, Neil, 1987, *Anti-Realism and Logic*, Oxford: Clarendon Press.

Turing, A.M., 1950, "Computing Machinery and Intelligence", *Mind*, vol. LIX(236).

Williams, D., 1992, *Nobody Nowhere: The Extraordinary Autobiography of an Autistic*, London: HarperCollins.

Wilson, D. and D Sperbar, 1981, "On Grice's Theory of Conversation", in *Conversation and Discourse*, ed. P. Werth, London: Croom Helm.

———, 1986, "On Defining Relevance", in *Philosophical Grounds of Rationality*, ed. R. Grandy and R. Warner, Oxford: Clarendon Press.

Wispe, Lauren, 1991, *The Psychology of Empathy*, New York: Plenum Press.

Wittgenstein, L., 1939, *Lectures on the Foundations of Mathematics*, Cambridge.

———, 1956, *Remarks on the Foundations of Mathematics*, tr. G.E.M. Anscombe, Cambridge (MA), and London: The MIT Press.

———, 1958, *Philosophical Investigations*, tr. G.E.M. Anscombe, Oxford: Basil Blackwell.

———, 1961a, *Notebooks 1914-16*, tr. G. Anscombe, Oxford: Blackwell.

———, 1961b, *Tractatus Logico-Philosophicus*, tr. D.F. Pears and B.F. McGuinness, London and Henley: Routledge & Kegan Paul.

———, 1969, *On Certainty*, ed. G.E.M. Anscombe and G.H. von Wright, tr G.E.M. Anscombe and D. Paul, Oxford: Basil Blackwell.

———, 1973, *Philosophical Investigations*, ed. G.E.M. Anscombe and G.H. von Wright, tr. G.E.M. Anscombe, Oxford: Blackwell.

———, 1974, *Philosophical Grammar*, ed. R. Rhees, tr. A. Kenny, Oxford: Blackwell.

———, 1978, *Remarks on the Foundation of Mathematics*, ed. H.G. von Wright, R. Rhees and G.E.M. Anscombe, tr. G.E.M. Anscombe, Oxford: Blackwell.

———, 1993, *Philosophical Occasions*, ed. J. Klagge and A. Nordmann, Indianapolis: Hackett.

Wright, C., 1980, *Wittgenstein on the Foundations of Mathematics*, London: Duckworth.

Zeki, Semir, 2003, "The Disunity of Consciousness", *Trends in Cognitive Science*, 7(5).

Index